D0122948

Lost in
Death
Valley

The True Story
of Four Families
in California's
Gold Rush

BY CONNIE GOLDSMITH

Twenty-First Century Books
Brookfield, Connecticut

With love to my sister Kerri Wright Wagner,
who always believed in me

Thanks to my critique partners on this book: Louise Monro Foley, Patricia M. Newman, and Tekla N. White for their valuable insight and advice, and to my editor, Dominic Barth, who pushed me on the details.

This book was made possible in part by a grant from the Society of Children's Book Writers and Illustrators.

Library of Congress Cataloging-in-Publication Data

Goldsmith, Connie, 1945-
   Lost in Death Valley : the true story of four families in California's gold rush / by Connie Goldsmith.
      p. cm.
Includes bibliographical references and index.
ISBN 0-7613-1915-8 (lib. bdg.)
1. Pioneers-California-Biography-Juvenile literature. 2. Pioneers-Death Valley (Calif. and Nev.)-Biography-Juvenile literature. 3. Frontier and pioneer life-California-Juvenile literature. 4. Frontier and pioneer life-Death Valley (Calif. and Nev.)-Juvenile literature. 5. California-Gold discoveries-Juvenile literature. 6. Overland journeys to the Pacific-Juvenile literature. 7. Desert survival-Death Valley (Calif. and Nev.)-History-19th century-Juvenile literature. 8. California-Biography-Juvenile literature 9. Death Valley (Calif. and Nev.)-Biography-Juvenile literature. [1. Overland journeys to the Pacific. 2. Frontier and pioneer life-Death Valley (Calif. and Nev.) 3. Desert survival. 4. California-Gold discoveries.] I. Title.

F865 .G685 2001
979.4'04'0922-dc21   00-057774

Published by Twenty-First Century Books
A Division of The Millbrook Press, Inc.
2 Old New Milford Road
Brookfield, Connecticut 06804
www.millbrookpress.com

CONTENTS

Note to the Reader

This is a true story. All the people in this book
actually lived. All the events retold actually
happened. All the quotations come from journals,
letters, books, or newspaper stories written
by the survivors, or interviews with them
or their descendants.

Sutter's Mill, California, where John Augustus Sutter found gold and started the gold rush.

GOLD FOUND IN CALIFORNIA

"GOLD! GOLD!" a man shouted in the streets of San Francisco. "Gold from the American river!"[1] It took nearly a year for news of the discovery of gold at Sutter's Mill, some 50 miles (80 km) northeast of Sacramento, California, on January 24, 1848, to reach the rest of the world. By 1849 the Gold Rush was on, and thousands of people streamed into California looking for their share. Most of the gold seekers came from other parts of the United States, but nearly a fourth of them came from Europe, China, and Latin America.

People have always valued gold because of its beauty and rarity. It is resistant to corrosion and easy to form into objects. Gold coins have been used as money for centuries, and the discovery of a new source of the metal was certain to attract a lot of attention.

Today it's hard to imagine how the discovery of gold affected people around the young nation. San Francisco almost became a ghost town when most of its people hurried to Sacramento to prospect for gold. In 1849, over 30,000 people traveled west on the trail from St. Louis.[2] One observer reported 500 wagons passing by in just three days.[3] The California Gold Rush began one of history's greatest migrations of people. The pioneers who journeyed to California during the Gold Rush in 1849 were called the forty-niners. Some of the pioneers, like ministers and teachers, were well educated. Others could barely read or write.

Most of the forty-niners coming from the country's East Coast traveled by sea to Panama or Nicaragua, crossed to the Pacific, and then sailed north. Others took a ship around the tip of South America. Those from the Midwest usually took the well-traveled Oregon Trail, across the Missouri River, through Nebraska and Wyoming, and into Salt Lake City, Utah. From there, the forty-niners followed the California Trail over the Sierra Nevada into the goldfields around Sacramento. Some used the Santa Fe Trail, a more southerly route that intersected with the Old Spanish Trail to Los Angeles.

Written guides for wagon-train travelers advised taking 150 pounds (86 kg) of flour or its equivalent in bread and 25 pounds (11 kg)of bacon and sugar for each person.[4] Food came dried or packed in tin cans. Eggs buried in cornmeal stayed fresh for weeks. Dried apples and raisins added a much needed sweet treat to the bland diet. And when fresh vegetables were not available, a few lemons carried along would prevent scurvy.

Recommended clothing included six pairs of socks, two pairs of underpants, one poncho, one coat, one overcoat, and high boots to protect legs from snakes. Soap, a comb, and a toothbrush were also needed.[5] Blankets and featherbeds provided warmth on cold nights. Families tried to bring a few personal items with them, jammed into the crush of necessary supplies. Well-off families carried enough clothing and fabric to last each growing child for years.

During the day, everyone had work to do. The men hunted for food, scouted the route ahead, and tended to the animals and wagons. Women not only looked after their own

An 1849 engraving of a wagon train of gold-seekers

families, they also cooked for the hired single men who often joined their mess—the name for a group of people traveling and eating together. The women cooked enough food each morning for a hot breakfast and a cold lunch. The usual meal was bread, bacon, beans, and coffee. Women's work included unpacking and repacking the wagons each day, mending clothing, and doing the laundry by hand.

Children helped with the animals, watched younger brothers and sisters, gathered wood, and milked the dairy cows that traveled with the wagon train. The "nooning" meal break gave children a chance to run around the wagons, making friends with other boys and girls. Mothers might give lessons in the evenings to the children using books, writing slates, paper, and pencils carried with them from back home.

Most people walked beside their wagons. A few traveled on horseback to help control the cattle. Only the elderly, the sick, and women with very young children rode in the cramped wagons, bumping over hard rocks, jerking up and down and sideways, causing motion sickness for those riding in them.

At night, the single men rolled up in blankets and slept under wagons or by campfires. If there was room, women slept in the wagons with their children. Many of the families had tents, and children enjoyed sleeping in them. Nighttime brought storytelling, music, and dancing around the campfires. Fiddles, harmonicas, and squeezebox accordions played songs we still sing today, like "Carry Me Back" and "Oh, Susanna." A well-known song of the time celebrated the excitement of the Gold Rush to California:

Then Ho! boys Ho! and to California go;
There's plenty of gold in the world untold,
On the banks of the Sacramento.[6]

CHAPTER 1

THE LURE OF GOLD

THOUSANDS OF CHILDREN traveled west with their parents during the Gold Rush. This is the story of four families who were part of a group of forty-niners that gathered in Salt Lake City, Utah, late in the summer of 1849. The families and their 11 children all had one thing in common—they'd given up their comfortable homes for the promise of gold that lured them west to a new life in California.

The Briers

Gold fever could strike anyone, even a circuit-riding Methodist minister in Iowa. The Reverend James Brier was a big, rawboned man, nearly six feet (1.83 m) tall and weighing 175 pounds (79 kg), with fair skin, brown-blond hair, and blue-gray eyes. His Scottish and Irish ancestors had given him the love for words so important to a good preacher.

Juliet Brier, a small woman just over five feet (1.52 m) tall and weighing 115 pounds (52 kg), had a gentle face, red-brown hair, and hazel eyes. She was a woman of great spiritual strength, and was deeply devoted to her husband. Juliet taught school before her three sons were born. In the summer when school let out, she often traveled with Reverend Brier as he made his church rounds.

Juliet Wells Brier, schooled in a Vermont seminary for ladies, was a religious woman. She was happy in Iowa, but

The Brier family in 1852: (left to right) Juliet, Columbus, James, and John, with Kirk in front

Reverend Brier was determined to go to California and prospect for gold. "I knew before starting we would have to suffer, but my husband wanted to go, and he needed me," Juliet wrote.[1]

Wives were expected to accept decisions made by their husbands, even if it meant never seeing their own family members again. A few months before leaving for California Juliet Brier wrote a letter to her brother, Hiram Wells. "The children talk a great deal about you. You never saw three more healthy, rosy and active children. I know that we shall not meet again on earth, but remember me in your prayers, and write often."[2]

Reverend Brier caught gold fever. Without talking with Juliet, he sold the family house and farm animals to purchase a wagon and oxen for the trip west.

Reverend Brier left Iowa with his wife and three sons for Salt Lake City in the spring of 1849. When the Briers reached Utah, Columbus, the oldest boy, was eight years old, John was six, and Kirk was four. Juliet Brier probably gave grammar, geography, and math lessons to Columbus and John. The children also received regular Bible lessons. Education was important to the family.

Juliet Brier brought along family albums and a wooden chest full of valuable silverware, a wedding gift from her parents. Reverend Brier carried his Bible and other favorite books with him. Their wagon was stuffed full of supplies and clothing. They felt prepared for anything the future might hold.

The Bennetts, William Manly, and John Rogers

On February 2, 1849, the *Wisconsin Tribune* told of inexhaustible supplies of gold in California. A soldier reported seeing "lumps of gold weighing one and two pounds (28.3

Martha Bennett　　　　　　　　Asabel Bennett

and 56.6 g), hearing of lumps weighing sixteen and twenty-five pounds (7.26 and 11.35 kg)."[3] The newspaper offered advice on how to construct a wagon, and talked about what animals and supplies to take on a trip to California. It seemed that the only cure for gold fever was a trip to the land of fabled wealth.

No wonder the fur trader Asabel Bennett, thirty-six, decided to try his luck in the Gold Rush! He sold his farm, and made plans to take his family to California in the spring. Asabel and his wife, twenty-five-year-old Sarah, left Wisconsin in May 1849 with their three children, eight-year-old George, five-year-old Melissa, and, two-year-old Martha. Bennett took two wagons, driving one himself and hiring a teamster to drive the other. The Bennetts' dog Cuff, an 80-pound (36.3-kg) greyhound and mastiff mix, traveled with them.

William Lewis Manly

William Manly, a good friend of the Bennetts, planned to go west with them. He was a short, sturdy man of twenty-eight who'd hunted, trapped, and farmed. Manly was away trying to buy a horse for the trip when the Bennetts unexpectedly set off for Salt Lake City without him. The cattle would need to graze the best springtime grass as they traveled, and Bennett felt he couldn't wait for Manly.

Bennett left a note for Manly saying they'd meet at Council Bluffs, the main crossing on the Missouri River. The Bennetts traveled with the Moody and Skinner families, neighbors from their home town. Families and friends often journeyed west together for safety and companionship. In early October 1849, the Bennetts joined the large wagon train near Salt Lake City, where they waited with 400 other forty-niners to head for California.

When William Manly got Bennett's message about the early departure, Manly and his new friend John Rogers left Wisconsin in a hurry, trying to catch up with the Bennetts. John Rogers was twenty-six and hailed from Tennessee. Called "Giant John" by his friends, Rogers towered well over six feet (1.83 m), very tall for those days.

But it would be a long time and a thousand miles (1,609 km) before the young men caught up to the Bennetts. When Manly and Rogers reached Council Bluffs, they discovered the Bennetts hadn't been there. The Missouri River had been too rough at that point, and the Bennett family had crossed the river at a place named Kanesville instead.

Four months later, when Manly and Rogers reached Salt Lake City, they were eager to join up with a wagon train. William Manly set out to find someone in charge who could give them permission. He could scarcely believe his luck when he spotted Sarah Bennett sitting in the family wagon.

Bennett had carried Manly's gear and money with him to Utah in the hopes of meeting his young friend again. The Bennetts asked both Manly and Rogers to join their mess. Bennett told them, "You need not do any work. You just look around and kill what game you can for us."[4] Now the Bennetts, too, were ready to move on toward California.

The Arcans

In the spring of 1849, Jean Arcan and his wife, Abigail, also decided to head for California. Arcan was skilled in gun-smithing and carpentry, important trades for a new territory. Their son Charles was only one-and-a-half when the Arcans set out on the long road to Salt Lake City. They traveled with two wagons and hired teamsters to help drive them.

Like so many others, the Arcans joined the large wagon train gathered in Salt Lake City in late September. They met

Abigail Arcan

Jean Arcan

Charlie Arcan posing as a swimming instructor at the
Neptune Baths in Santa Cruz, California. He was one-
and-a-half years old when the journey west began.

the Bennett family there and became good friends. The Arcans traveled with the Bennetts from then on, never parting company until the end of their journey.

The Wades

Englishman Henry Wade had been a coachman for the King of England. Mary, his wife, had tutored the French Ambassador's children in London. In 1835 their first child, Harry George, was born in England. Baby Harry was only two weeks old when Henry Wade suddenly announced to his wife, "Mary, get everything packed to leave in a week. I have tickets for New York."[5] English wives had no more say about their futures than did American wives. The Wades had three other children in America.

Gold Rush fever hit the Wades early in 1849. Henry traded his farm for ox teams and wagons. On April 1, he set off for Salt Lake City with Mary and their four children. Harry was fourteen by then and old enough to do a man's work. He could drive the team nearly as well as his father. His younger siblings were Charles, twelve, Almira, nine, and Richard, five. The Wades also joined the big wagon train in Utah.

The four families—the Briers, Bennetts, Arcans, and Wades—waited in Salt Lake City for the weather to cool, planning the rest of their trip to California to build their new lives with the gold they hoped to find.

Harry Wade

Mary Wade

Richard Wade was five years old on the journey through Death Valley.

Almira Wade was nine years old when her family headed west.

Salt Lake City, Utah, circa 1850

CHAPTER 2

THE SAND WALKING COMPANY

IN 1849, SALT LAKE CITY was a thriving village built around a fort. Brigham Young, the leader of the Mormon Church, led his people there to escape religious persecution. People lived in small log cabins and adobe houses with vegetable gardens. Covered wagons served as extra bedrooms. Wooden fences lined wide, dusty streets, and small farms with herds of cows surrounded the town.

By September 1849, hundreds of gold seekers crowded into Salt Lake City. They milled about, buying supplies and trying to decide on the best route to California. After the disaster of the Donner Party in 1846, people feared trying to cross the mountains too late in the fall. Early blizzards had surprised the Donner Party in the Sierra Nevada during the winter as they crossed an uncharted shortcut. Forty-two people died of starvation trapped in snow-covered shacks. Rumors about the disaster leading to cannibalism haunted the western trails for years. No one who traveled to California could forget that story.

Wintering over in Salt Lake City wasn't practical, because the hundreds of waiting gold seekers had depleted the town's food supplies. Citizens worried about running short of food during coming months. Brigham Young was eager for the forty-niners to leave Salt Lake City before winter arrived. He recommended the Old Spanish Trail, which ran from Santa Fe to Los Angeles. The forty-niners would have to go south from Utah to pick up the trail. From there, they would travel west to Los Angeles, then north to Sacramento and the mother lode.

The Old Spanish Trail was a longer route to California than across the Sierra, but it was well traveled. The Spanish Catholic priests had used it for years to communicate with the Spanish California missions. The Mormons also used parts of the trail to reach roadsteads in Southern California where their new converts arrived.

In late September, the Briers, Bennetts, Arcans, and Wades, along with hundreds of other gold seekers, left Salt Lake City. They congregated at Hobble Creek, a stream running through wild flax fields just south of town. During nighttime campfire meetings, people argued about which way to go. Should they risk crossing the Sierra on the California Trail before winter set in? Or should they try the Old Spanish Trail to the south? After days of debate, the members of the wagon trains opted for the southern route.

Organization came next. Wagon training was serious business, and most big wagon trains formed a company. The men at Hobble Creek elected leaders and signed contracts describing the rules that would govern them during the journey. They agreed to help one another if someone lost a wagon, or if food and supplies ran short.

Men of the wagon train named themselves the "San Joaquin Company" after California's rich central valley. But most people didn't know Spanish and didn't understand the words. They started using the prophetic nickname "Sand Walking Company." The Company further broke up into seven smaller divisions, with names like Jayhawkers,

Captain Jefferson Hunt

Mississippi Boys, Georgians, Hawkeyes, and Wolverines. The Briers joined the Mississippi Boys, and the other three families joined the Jayhawkers.

None of the Sand Walkers knew how to get to the Old Spanish Trail, so they needed a guide. The Company hired Captain Jefferson Hunt, a veteran of the Mexican War. He'd traveled the Old Spanish Trail before and knew it well. Captain Hunt agreed to lead the Company to Los Angeles. The trip would take nine weeks. He charged the Sand Walking Company $10 per wagon, a reasonable fee considering his experience.

Captain Hunt was a respected Mormon Elder. To many of the forty-niners, though, he appeared silent and withdrawn. Six-year-old John Brier feared the white-haired, grim-looking guide and later wrote, "I confess that I was afraid of the silent man, and wondered if he ever loved anybody, and if he slept on horseback."[1]

Captain Hunt told the Sand Walkers that only one wagon had ever crossed the Old Spanish Trail before; it had been used primarily by men on horseback. He warned them about the scarcity of water and food for the animals. He said that some of the cattle would die along the way. In spite of these dangers, Captain Hunt agreed with the Company's decision. Traveling the Old Spanish Trail was safer than starting across the Sierra in October.

The Sand Walkers set off from Hobble Creek, Utah, on October 3, 1849. The 107 wagons raised clouds of dust along the mile-long train, with 400 men, women, and children plodding along in the dirt. Food and supplies filled the wagons; wooden barrels of water hung outside. It took at least four trained oxen to pull each wagon. Milk cows and mules also tagged along. About 1,000 animals accompanied the huge wagon train.

The men took turns riding out front to break the trail. Being in front meant a tough day of forging a path through thick brush. Being in back meant eating dirt and breathing the dust thrown up by animals and people moving ahead. A gooey paste of sweat and dirt covered faces and clothing after a few hours. Depending on the terrain, an average day's journey was four to fourteen miles. Devices to count miles were mounted on the spokes of the iron wagon wheels.

Each division rotated nighttime guard duty for the wagon train, one night the Jayhawkers, the Mississippi Boys the next. Sometimes the churchgoing folk asked Reverend Brier or one of the religious men in the wagon train to lead them in prayers at the end of the evening. Spirits soared at the start of the journey, and strangers quickly became good friends. The trip promised to be the adventure of a lifetime.

CHAPTER 3

A Mysterious Indian Map

THE TRAIL THE SAND WALKERS followed from Hobble Creek crossed high desert plains, where sagebrush replaced trees. Thin grass fed the cattle; sage hens and plentiful jackrabbits became stew for hungry people. "The country was alive with bunnies," wrote one traveler.[1]

On October 18, 1849, a weathered-looking man named Captain Wesley Smith overtook the Sand Walking Company. He carried a map of a shortcut across the mountains to California. The map promised to cut 500 miles (805 km) and 20 days off the trip, and it showed grass and water all the way to California. The map supposedly was copied from one drawn in the sand by the great Ute chief Walkara, head of the Timpanogots Ute band that controlled parts of the present state of Utah during its Mexican and early American phases.

William Manly and John Rogers, the two young bachelors traveling with the Bennett family, knew Chief Walkara. He'd saved their lives months before as they'd floated down Utah's Green River on a sinking raft, trying to reach California. Chief Walkara was aware of Mormons as a rising power in his world. When Manly and Rogers told Walkara that they were Mormon (although they weren't), he'd shown the men the way to Salt Lake City. Manly and Rogers told the Sand Walkers that Chief Walkara was an honorable man, and that his map could be trusted.

The Sand Walkers argued about what route to take to California. Some of them started to doubt Captain Hunt's ability to lead them. The Christians suspected that the Mormons tricked them into leaving Salt Lake City because food was running short. Others said that the Mormons were using the forty-niners to forge a better trail to California—a route the Mormons used to reach their new outpost at San Bernardino.

The possibility of a shortcut appealed to the Sand Walkers. What should they do? Should they take the short-cut shown on the map, trusting that it was accurate? Or should they keep to the Old Spanish Trail, a known road, but 500 miles (805 km) longer? They had two weeks to decide before reaching the cutoff point, and travel was getting tougher each day.

One Sand Walker wrote that Reverend Brier was a "fellow that liked to give his opinion on every subject. When the crowd came together, he was called on to make the first speech."[2] There were other preachers in the group, but Reverend Brier always seemed to speak out first.

"Why should we go 500 miles (805 km) out of our way? The trail we're on now is so bad that no shortcut could be worse,"[3] argued Reverend Brier at one campfire meeting. "Go west! In six weeks we'll be loaded with gold!" he shouted.[4] "Sink or swim, live or die, I will take the cutoff, go it boots."[5]

Captain Hunt warned the Sand Walkers that it was dangerous to take the unknown route. He believed it wasn't safe for the women and children. "Gentlemen, all I have to say is that if you take that route you will all be landed in Hell."[6] But he was determined to uphold his end of the bargain. "I was hired to go by way of Los Angeles, but if you all wish to go and follow Smith I will go also. But if even one wagon decides to go the original route, I shall feel bound to go with that wagon."[7]

In the end, only seven wagons—including several Mormon missionaries bound for Hawaii by way of Los Angeles—continued south with Captain Hunt. Perhaps Manly's recommendation convinced these forty-niners to believe in the mysterious map rather than follow the advice of their experienced guide, Captain Hunt. Or maybe it was Reverend Brier's persuasive words.

The other forty-niners were so eager to get to the gold-fields that on November 4, 1849, 100 wagons turned west onto the unknown Indian trail, hoping for a shorter way to California. The Brier, Bennett, Arcan, and Wade families, along with Manly and Rogers, were among those that turned onto the shortcut.

But Captain Hunt's group would reach Los Angeles on December 22, 1849, many weeks ahead of those taking the shortcut. Captain Hunt's group would retain their wagons and possessions. They would have a happy and safe Christmas while their comrades struggled half-starved in Death Valley. And everyone in Captain Hunt's group would still be alive.

For two days the trail along the shortcut headed up into pleasant rolling hills, with plenty of water and grass for the animals. It was early November, but winter hadn't yet arrived. On the third day the wagon train climbed a summit covered with junipers. A narrow trail snaked down into the gorge on the other side of the mountain. The travelers found themselves boxed into a canyon that towered 1,000 feet (305 m) high.

Manly worried about the route ahead. "In front of us was a canyon, impassable for wagons. Men could go, perhaps horses and mules, but wagons could no longer follow that trail."[8] Scouts rode out to look for a way across the deep canyon. They returned with bad news. There was no way through for the wagons.

"Gloom settled like a pall over the camp, and the only revenge they could find for their miseries was in naming the place Mount Misery."[9] Disillusioned, the people of 73 wagons turned back to catch up with Captain Hunt's group. They never caught up, but they were able to follow Hunt's tracks to the Old Spanish Trail and then to Los Angeles.

The Bennetts' Midwest neighbors, the Moody and Skinner families, turned back with the larger group of wagons. They were afraid to continue on the unknown shortcut. The Briers, along with the Bennetts, Arcans, and Wades, waited at Mount Misery, hoping to discover a way out of the canyon that their wagons could navigate.

John Brier later wrote that only one person—an unnamed Canadian—managed to climb down the cliffs to the stream at Mount Misery. The man brought up buckets of water to sell to his fellow travelers. "Those who drank of his water were compelled to pay at the rate of one dollar per bucket," John said.[10]

Finally the last scout returned with word of a way out for the wagons along the rim of the canyon through an evergreen forest. John Brier described that canyon passage. "Ax-men led the way and the silence of ages was broken by sounds familiar to the logging camps of Maine. A rough and hazardous track was exposed which tested the discipline of the oxen and the will of the drivers."[11]

And so the remaining 27 wagons and about 85 people agreed to keep on traveling west along the supposed shortcut. "We will follow this trail or leave our bones on the way," declared a Jayhawker named Stephens.[12] Only four families continued as part of the smaller wagon train—the Briers, Bennetts, Arcans, and Wades. The rest were single men, some traveling in groups like the Jayhawkers, and some traveling with the families as hired hands.

The first death among the Sand Walkers occurred near Mount Misery. A Kentucky man who had been sick when he started the trip, died. It was Sunday, and the wagon train usually halted on the Sabbath for rest and religious services. To mark the death of the unfortunate traveler, Reverend Brier gave a sermon titled: "There Shall Be No More Death."[13] But he was wrong.

CHAPTER 4

THE FAMILIES SPLIT UP

IT WASN'T LONG before the single men began to see the women and children as burdens. The families had heavier wagons and herded more cattle with them. The women and children couldn't walk as far in a day as the men. The Jayhawkers told the families to follow Captain Hunt's trail where they could travel together at a slower pace. The men elected a new leader, then ejected the four families from what was left of the Sand Walking Company.

But Reverend Brier wouldn't let his family be left behind. He insisted on following the Jayhawkers. "I shall not bother nor detain you, but only wish to travel in the wake of your train."[1]

The Jayhawkers reluctantly agreed to allow the Briers to travel with them, but made it clear they came along at their own risk. One wrote, "Reverend Brier and Family came up and wanted to travel with us. At first we objected, as we didn't want to be encumbered with women, but we hadn't the heart to refuse."[2]

And so the wagon train split up again. The last place the four families camped together was at Papoose Lake, a salty, slimy body of unpotable water. The next morning, the Briers set off, trailing the Jayhawkers on the imagined shortcut, even though they were unwelcome. Juliet Brier might have wished to go with the other three families, but she always supported her husband's decisions.

Some accounts tell of a pony that Juliet rode with her youngest children, John and Kirk.[3] But it ran away or was stolen early in the journey. The Brier family would have to follow the Jayhawkers on foot.

The Bennetts, Arcans, and Wades thought it best for their families to stick together. They continued with Manly and Rogers, looking for their own route into California. A few of the older men also took their wagons and traveled with the families rather than race through the wilderness after the young Jayhawkers. All followed the same general route, headed southwest toward Los Angeles.

William Manly could have joined the rest of the Jayhawkers and forged ahead with the single men. He later wrote about his decision. "If I were alone with no one to expect me to help them, I would be out before any other man, but with women and children in the party, to go and leave them would be to pile everlasting infamy on my head. The thought almost made me crazy, but I thought it would be better to stay and die with them, bravely struggling to escape than to forsake them in their weakness."[4] Manly would stick with the Bennetts and Arcans. And where Manly went, so went his friend, John Rogers.

Manly spent most of his time scouting ahead for water and the best way through the mountains. Jean Arcan owned a telescope that Manly carried. Manly often camped alone at night, away from the others with only his compass, a rifle, a blanket, and his horse for company. Sometimes he ran into the Jayhawkers or one of the other divisions as they also looked for the best route across the endless mountains and valleys.

Manly took his telescope to the highest summit "and scanned the country very carefully, especially to the west and north, and found it very barren. There were no trees, no fertile valleys, nor anything green. Away to the west some mountains stood out clear, their summits covered white with snow."[5] Manly concluded about this time that taking the shortcut shown on the so-called Walkara map had been a mistake. But all were now committed, and there was no turning back.

Grass and water became scarce, and the oxen suffered as much as the people did. "Though fat and sleek when we started from Salt Lake, they now looked gaunt and poor, and dragged themselves slowly along, poor faithful servants of mankind."[6] Everyone knew that when the oxen could go no further, they would have to be killed and used for food. A skinny ox provided less than 50 pounds (23 kg) of meat, and it tasted bitter from the animal's sagebrush diet.

One night as Manly camped alone, he built a small fire to warm himself. "I thought it looked dark and troublesome before us," he said. "I took a stone for a pillow with my hat on it for a cushion, and lying down close under the shelving rock, I went to sleep."[7]

He reported crying lonely, bitter tears of worry. "I felt I should be morally guilty of murder if I should forsake Mr. Bennett's wife and children, and the family of Mr. Arcan with whom I had been associated. I got around to the determination to stand by my friends, their wives and children, come what might."[8] Manly's allegiance was to his friends, the Bennetts and Arcans, not to the Wades or Briers.

The Wades had traveled with the Sand Walkers from Utah, and they took the proposed shortcut along with the Bennett, Arcan, and Brier families. They usually traveled a day behind the Bennetts and Arcans and were seldom seen.

The Wades had had little contact with the other three families, and were never considered part of their group.

Following the trail broken by those ahead meant that the Wade wagons had an easier time of it during the journey. Henry Wade's work as an English coachman made him the most experienced wagon driver of the Death Valley forty-niners. He also had strong opinions, and "handled his team as he would have handled a coach and four for the king."[9] Some men found Wade's manners arrogant. He wasn't popular with others in the wagon train, who had far less skill at driving teams than he did.

Perhaps because the Wades trailed the others, no one knew them well. Almira Wade had been nine years old during the journey. She told a newspaper reporter years later why her father insisted on lagging behind. "There was an ever increasing dearth of good water and feed. My father tried to keep about a day behind the rest so that by giving the small springs time to refill, there would be water enough for them all."[10]

Neither the Bennetts nor the Arcans ever wrote about their journey. Manly, who was with them for much of it, wrote a book that became famous and many letters and articles about his experiences in Death Valley, as did the Briers and several of the Jayhawkers. Most of what happened to the Bennetts and Arcans has been reported through Manly's eyes.

Sarah Bennett once overheard her husband talking with Manly about their dismal prospects. She cried, fearful that her children would die of thirst and starvation. Their hunger was temporarily relieved when one of the men "found a small pile of squashes covered over with sagebrush. They had divided them in camp and all were eaten with relish, as they were very good."[11]

The Bennett-Arcan party was still in the high desert where it is quite cold in winter. One night, a few inches of snow fell. "When daylight came, the oxen crowded around the wagons, shivering with cold, and licking up the snow to quench their thirst."[12] All the cooking pots were filled with snow to melt for drinking water.

The weak oxen could no longer pull the heavy wagons. The families began dumping their heaviest possessions, like furniture and books, along the trail. Manly said, "Mr. Bennett was a carpenter and had brought along some good tools in his wagon. These he reluctantly unloaded and almost everything else, except bedding and provisions, and leaving them upon the ground, we rolled up the hills slowly, with loads as light as possible."[13]

Rogers and Manly continued to scout ahead of the group. One day they found an Indian family that gave them a handful of corn. The Indians also showed them where a warm spring bubbled from the ground. The men hurried back to the family wagons to share the bounty.

At the camp, Manly found Sarah Bennett and Abigail Arcan "in heart-rending distress. The four children were crying for water but there was not a drop to give them, and none could be reached before some time next day. The mothers were nearly crazy, for they expected the children would choke with thirst and die in their arms, and they would rather perish themselves than suffer the agony of seeing their little ones gasp and slowly die."[14]

The women were sorry they'd come on the journey. "They reproached themselves as being the cause of all this trouble. For the love of gold they had left homes where hunger had never come."[15] The corn and canteens of water that Manly brought them relieved their hunger and thirst. "There were tears of thankfulness and joy on their cheeks as they blessed us over and over again."[16]

One of the stringy oxen was slaughtered, and its meat put on a slow fire to cook overnight. Some hours later, Bennett found the meat had been stolen. By someone in the camp? By an Indian? "It is a sort of unwritten law that in parties such as ours, he who steals provisions forfeits his life."[17] Bennett and Manly never discovered the thief, but they kept a closer watch on their food after that.

The Bennett-Arcan party continued on, struggling from water hole to water hole, suffering from hunger and thirst. The men ate only the dried meat from the stringy oxen, saving the rice and flour for the women and children. Seven wagons now composed their mess, four belonging to the Bennett and Arcan families, and the other three belonging to the few single men who still traveled with them. As before, the party was following the trail of the Jayhawkers and the Briers, who traveled a little faster. And the Wade family in turn, traveled a day behind the Bennetts and Arcans.

There was no one to show the families the way. There was no one to tell them how much farther they had to go, no one to point out the next water hole. There was only the belief that Los Angeles lay to the southwest, and that they must keep going in that direction, no matter what.

CHAPTER 5

ACROSS THE HIGH DESERT

THE UTAH TERRITORY EXTENDED all the way to California in 1849 and included what are now the states of Utah and Nevada. The Briers and Jayhawkers trekked across dry, barren deserts sliced by mountain ranges running north to south. Wary Indians often watched the Sand Walkers from high cliffs.

For about five weeks the Briers and their three boys trailed the Jayhawkers, sometimes camping with them, sometimes traveling alone. The Jayhawkers themselves included remnants of other divisions of the Sand Walkers—the Mississippi Boys, with three slaves (known only as Little West, Tom, and Joe), and the Georgians, nicknamed the Bug Smashers.

Meeting, then splitting up, and rejoining each other again, the Briers and the small clumps of men lost all semblance of an organized company. Each group made its own way across the terrible desert; each man looked out for himself and his friends.

One day the Jayhawkers captured two Indian men. Using sign language, they told the Indians that the travelers needed water. The Indians led the men to water, then both of them managed to escape their captors. This surprised the forty-niners, who felt they'd treated the Indians with kindness. One

The Sand Walkers passed through what are now secret military lands—the Nevada Test Site, Nellis Air Force Range, and the mysterious Area 51. You cannot photograph these areas. They traveled north of today's Las Vegas and Lake Mead, created when Hoover Dam confined the Colorado River.

writer later speculated that if the Jayhawkers had given gifts to the Indians instead of capturing them, Indian guides might have led them safely through the desert.

The Death Valley forty-niners stood at the top of each mountain, gazing westward, expecting to see the Pacific Ocean. Instead, they saw only more desolate land ahead. Barren mountains and treeless valleys loomed in all directions. Great bleak peaks speared the cloudless sky. Sand, dusty sagebrush, and rocks posed obstacles for wagon wheels. Distant dried-up lake beds caked with clay gleamed in the sunlight, falsely promising fresh water.

But day after day the Briers and Jayhawkers pushed on, even though water was scarce and food began to run out. The only supply in abundance was coffee. Even the children drank boiled coffee to help hide the taste of the muddy, bitter water they found.

The remaining oxen grew thin and weak and could barely pull the heavy wooden wagons. Blood stained their footprints as the rocky ground tore their tender feet. The animals ground and gnashed their teeth in hungry frustration. They moaned for water like hopeless humans.

The Briers and Jayhawkers found a huge flat lake only half an inch deep. The men dug holes into the lake bed so water could seep in and fill them. It took hours of work to scoop out enough water for the thirsty people and desperate cattle.

The Amargosa Desert, Nevada, with Charleston Peak in the distance

Reverend Brier came down with dysentery. By the end of the trip, he would lose 100 pounds (45 kg) from his large-boned frame. John Brier wrote, "My father had always been active and enterprising. He'd spent his manhood in self-sacrificing labor and had never known what it meant to be discouraged. Now, we could see that he was failing. . . . It was hard for him to perform ordinary duties of the camp. Still, he continued to explore as he'd always done, until his infirmity forced him to the rear."[1]

At Forty Mile Canyon, where southwest Nevada meets California in the heart of the Amargosa Desert, the Briers abandoned their wagon. The mountains loomed too high and the canyons too deep and narrow for its passage. The oxen could no longer pull the heavy wagon through the soft sand and across the hard rocks. "It was a fatal step," wrote Juliet Brier, "as we were about 500 miles (805 km) from Los Angeles and had only our feet to take us there."[2]

People made difficult decisions about what to keep. The oxen were trained to pull heavy loads, but they could also carry supplies in backpacks made from the wagon canvas. Anything that couldn't fit into the backpacks had to be left behind.

Juliet buried her beloved silverware and abandoned the treasured family picture albums. She discarded piles of her children's clothing. Even the white tent the family had been sleeping in was dumped. Everything needed to start a new life in a new land had been carried along in the wagons. It devastated the travelers to leave nearly all of their belongings and household goods behind in the desert.

Years later, John Brier wrote about that time, describing those things remembered from youth: "The drifting sand, the cold blast from the north, the wind-beaten hill, the white tent, my lesson in the Testament, the burning of wagons as fuel, the forsaking of nearly every treasured thing, the packing of oxen and the melancholy departure."[3]

Some of the Jayhawkers chopped their wagons in half, turning them into small two-wheeled carts that were easier for the oxen to pull. The men hammered out new shoes from the iron wagon wheels for the animals' painful feet. They slaughtered the weakest ox, and dried its meat into beef jerky over fires built by burning leftover pieces of the wooden wagons. Water, food, and guns were jammed into the backpacks and loaded onto the oxen.

Indians collected some of the goods abandoned by the Death Valley forty-niners. Later pioneers and historians picked up the rest, sometimes placing the artifacts in museums. If an object could be traced to a particular person, it might be returned.

One observer wrote that the only water to be found came from tiny seeps at the base of canyon walls. The travelers found that the Indians had made little cups of clay to catch the water as it slowly dripped down the canyon face, but this provided enough water only for the people.

The oxen suffered greatly from thirst and hunger. "The poor cattle crowded around the men with heads low, and hollow-eyed as if they actually begged for something to eat and drink."[4] As soon as one of the weakened oxen died of thirst or hunger, it was butchered for food, and its hide used for moccasins. The surviving oxen also got hide shoes to help protect their sore feet from jagged stones.

Because the oxen were a traveling food supply, it was important to keep them alive as long as possible. Once the cattle were gone, there would be no more food.

The weary travelers trudged out of the Amargosa Desert, then up and into the gray Funeral Mountains. The 40 or 50 men struggled in small clusters, with long distances between each group. The Briers continued to trail at the end.

Juliet Brier described the days just before the family entered Death Valley on foot. "The ground was hard and composed of small pieces of broken rock. Night came and no water all day long. I'd walked in silence, not in sight or hearing of a soul except my little ones."[5]

The Funeral Mountains

Sometimes Juliet carried John on her back and held Kirk in her arms. "Oh, Mama, could you carry me a little?" Kirk would cry. She would carry him a few minutes. Then he would say, "I can walk now." A moment later it was, "I'm tired. I can't walk."[6] On some days, there was no water at all for the children. There was no water for anyone.

CHAPTER 6

CHRISTMAS IN DEATH VALLEY

JULIET BRIER STOOD HIGH in the Funeral Mountains staring at the nightmare landscape spread out below her west to Death Valley. "Oh, what a desolate country we looked down into . . . The men said they could see what looked like springs out in the valley. Mr. Brier was always ahead to explore and find water, so I was left with our three little boys to bring up the cattle. We expected to reach the spring in a few hours, and the men pushed ahead. I was sick and weary, and the hope of a good camping place was all that kept me up."[1]

Death Valley is surrounded in all directions by mountain ranges. Because it blocked the way west, the forty-niners had no choice but to descend into it. At least six different groups of forty-niners made their way down to the valley floor over the next few days. The other three families, along with Manly and Rogers, followed two days behind the Briers and Jayhawkers. Although the travelers didn't realize it, they traced ancient game trails and Indian paths.

Juliet Brier wrote, "Many times I felt I should faint, and as my strength departed, I would sink to my knees. The boys would ask for water, but there was not a drop. Thus we staggered over salty wastes, trying to keep the Company in view. . . . I knew if we had stopped the men would come back at

Death Valley,
looking north toward
Furnace Creek

night for us, but I didn't want to be a drag or hindrance."[2]
Sometimes Kirk, the youngest Brier boy, rode uncomfortably
on the back of a ox, clinging to its saddlebags.

On Christmas Eve 1849, the Briers entered Death Valley.
Reverend Brier scouted far ahead with his cattle and the
other men, looking for water and a campsite. The cold night
air of the desert chilled Juliet and her three children as they

struggled alone in the dark. Juliet carried Kirk on her back. Her other children, Columbus and John, stumbled alongside. Only the crunch of their feet on the salty, dry sand broke the deep desert silence.

Juliet fell to her knees to search in the starlight for the ox tracks as she tried to follow the trail. She stood again, and went on for a few more minutes until she lost the trail once more. Kirk cried for water, but Juliet had none to give him. She didn't know if they would reach camp or die of thirst first.

About midnight the three children and their mother rounded a huge boulder and found Reverend Brier sitting at a small fire. "Is this the camp?" Juliet asked her husband.[3] She and her children had been walking since dawn. They were hungry and thirsty and tired beyond exhaustion.

"No, it's six miles (9.6 km) further," the Reverend Brier answered.[4] He scooped up Kirk and carried the little boy in his arms, while Juliet trudged behind with Columbus and John in tow.

At three o'clock on Christmas morning the Brier family reached the small camp. The men they traveled with slept near a roaring fire and freshwater springs. Juliet was worn out. "I only wanted to sleep, but my husband said I must eat and drink or I would never wake up."[5] A man called Mr. Masterson gave the Briers a few scraps of bread to eat. After deep drinks of water, the family fell asleep near the fire, sheltered by overhanging rock walls.

The next morning Juliet discovered that the camp was blessed with plenty of water. Cold springs provided the thirsty travelers and their cattle with all the water they wanted. Hot springs gave them a chance to wash dirty clothes and scrub filthy bodies. Green willow trees offered shade. And while there wasn't any food for the people, plentiful grass growing in the damp sand filled the bellies of their hungry cattle.

The men killed one of the scrawny oxen for Christmas dinner. Biscuits and black coffee completed the feast. Food was rationed because no one knew how much longer they would have to travel before finding more. They didn't even know if they were in California yet.

"It was a Christmas none could ever forget," Juliet said. "Music or singing? My, no. We were too far gone for that. Nobody spoke very much, but I knew we were all thinking of home back East, and all the cheer and good things there. Men would sit looking into the fire or stand gazing away silently over the mountains, and it was easy to read their thoughts. Poor fellows! Having no other woman here, I felt lonesome at times, but I was glad too, that no other was there to suffer.[6]

"There were no illuminations on Christmas Eve."[7] The Briers were grateful to still be alive. "My little ones had no thoughts of Santa Claus that year."[8]

Later that day, Reverend Brier lectured his sons about the value of a good education. William Manly, scouting ahead for the Bennetts and Arcans, caught up with the Briers on Christmas Day. He said, "When I arrived at the camp, I found the reverend gentleman very cooly delivering a lecture to his boys on education. It seemed very strange to me to hear a solemn discourse about education when starvation was staring us all in the face."[9]

Louis Nusbaumer, one of the young Jayhawkers camping in Death Valley on Christmas Day, wrote a letter to his wife, Lisette. She had remained behind in Germany, waiting for word from her husband. "I hope my dear wife is having a happier Christmas day than I am. Should I never return to her and should chance deliver this journal into her hands, she will glean from these pages that she was never far from my thoughts and my heart will beat for her to the last."[10]

One of the men, named Dr. Carr, asked Juliet, "Don't you think you and the children better remain here and let me send back for you?"[11]

"No," she said. "I have never been a hindrance. I have never kept the Company waiting, neither have my children, and every step I take will be toward California."[12] She knew that to wait in the desert for help could mean death for her children. "Give up? Oh, I knew what that meant; a shallow grave in the sand!"[13]

As the group gathered around the blazing campfire that evening, the men asked Reverend Brier to speak. He gave the speech about education that he'd practiced with his children that morning. Everyone cheered Reverend Brier's hopeful words. He prayed aloud with his family and the men as darkness fell. The first Christmas ever celebrated in Death Valley came to a close.

The Brier family and the men traveling with them fell asleep, hoping the worst of the three-month trip across deserts and over mountain ranges was past. The golden land of promise in California must be near. It had to be!

Death Valley is about 140 miles (225 km) long, and varies from 3 to 16 miles (5 to 25 km) wide. It is walled on each side by treacherous cliffs and mountains. The lowest spot at Badwater lies 280 feet (87 m) below sea level. The driest place in North America, Death Valley averages less than 2 inches (5 cm) of rain each year. Summer temperatures soar to 120°F (49°C) or more. Sand dunes, salt flats, and alkali marshes cover the valley floor.

Death Valley Through the Ages

Complex geological upheavals created Death Valley. Earthquakes and natural forces twisted and tilted layers of rocks. The crust of the earth itself sank, producing the flat desert floor that bakes between the Amargosa and Panamint mountain ranges. Volcanoes left black mountains and huge dark stones like lumps of coal.

Seas and lakes came and went over millions of years. During the Paleozoic period (600 to 225 million years ago), a warm, shallow sea covered Death Valley. Trilobites, snails, sponges, and seaweed flourished in the saline water. When the sea dried up, it left deep salt beds on the desert floor. In the Pleistocene Ice Ages (2.5 million to 5,000 years ago), a lake 100 miles (161 km) long and 600 feet (183 m) deep filled Death Valley. The lake grew and shrank with the advance and retreat of ice. Today the dry lake is named Lake Manly after William Lewis Manly.

Fossil mammals found in the oldest rocks show that a small three-toed horse and an animal related to the modern rhinoceros once lived in Death Valley. Later fossils and footprints prove camels, antelopes, and several other kinds of ancient horses also roamed the land.

A thousand years ago, the Shoshone Indians moved into Death Valley, sharing its southern fringes with the Paiute. They eked out a precarious living by gathering mesquite beans and pine nuts from the hills, and catching a few small animals and birds to eat. Tiny fish live in a warm, salty creek in Death Valley, and the Indians regularly scooped up the fish in baskets and feasted on them. The Paiute called the valley Tomesha—"ground afire."

CHAPTER 7

IN THE VALLEY
OF DEATH

THE BRIERS NEVER FORGOT that Christmas Day; the spot is now called Travertine Springs, near Furnace Creek in Death Valley, California. Reverend Brier estimated that his family had walked 46 miles (74 km) in 20 hours without water to reach the springs, a very long distance for three small boys.

No one knew what to expect. Juliet said, "Next morning, the company moved on over the sand to—nobody knew where."[1] Later that day, the group found an old Indian buried in the sand with only his head showing. "He was shriveled and bald, and looked like a mummy. He must have been a hundred and fifty years old!"[2] The men dug the ancient Indian out of the sand, fed him beef jerky, gave him water, and propped him up in the shade where his people could find him.

The Briers moved north, following the Jayhawkers' faint path along the east side of Death Valley. Loomis St. John and a young man known only as Patrick joined the Brier mess and stayed with them for the rest of the journey. The Briers shared their meager food supply and blankets in return for help with the oxen.

The small groups of people seeking their separate ways out of Death Valley sometimes camped together at night.

In 1939, an Indian told writer Carl Wheat that he remembered the incident from his early childhood. The Indians had deserted their camp, leaving an old man with a broken leg behind, hidden in the sand. The Indians followed the white travelers to see what they were doing, and to pick up discarded belongings. Their kindness to the old Indian surprised and pleased them. The tribe decided that the white men meant them no harm.[3]

One evening when William Manly camped with the Jayhawkers, he asked about Reverend Brier. "They told me his wife was the best man of the two. He is willing for us to do all the work. He follows in our broken road, takes the easiest place and only works with his tongue!"[4]

For years the surviving forty-niners disagreed about Reverend Brier's actions in Death Valley. Some thought him lazy and useless, while others realized he was ill and admired his courage for continuing. It was a common practice of the day to poke fun at ministers, but Juliet Brier never faltered in her devotion to her husband.

The land led off into a salty marsh. Juliet wrote, "We struggled through for miles and miles. Oh, it was terrible! We would sink to our shoe tops and as water gave out, we were nearly famished. I have heard [that] our tracks were found there twelve years later, still encrusted in the hardened salt."[5]

At a salt creek just past the marsh, the Jayhawkers stopped to burn the last of their wagons—the little half wagons they'd made from splitting the large ones. They decided to "pack their backs," leave the wagons and cattle, and continue on foot, taking only what they could carry. The

Jayhawkers dried strips of poor ox meat over the fire in preparation for a final assault on the desert. It was a sad and solemn day. That night the pitiful remnants of the Sand Walkers slept in scattered camps strewn across the desert floor like a broken string of giant wooden beads.

Another dry march across twenty miles (32.2 km) of sand dunes brought the Briers to the foot of the mountains at the north end of Death Valley. Sandy wind lashed their faces and eyes, making their thirst more extreme. They camped that night, "with hope almost gone and not a drop of water to relieve our parched lips and swollen tongues."[6] Juliet kept her fears to herself, trying not to worry her children.

Snow covering the nearby mountain tops saved their lives. Reverend Brier and some of the Jayhawkers clambered up the side of the mountain and brought back snow, frozen in thick flannel shirts. Everyone had all the water they wanted, and even the frenzied cattle got their share of the melted snow.

The men from Georgia who'd called themselves the Bug Smashers caught up, ready for a final desperate try across the high mountains known today as the Panamint Range. They asked Juliet Brier to bake up their flour into biscuits. She did, although it took her until midnight. The men gave Juliet a biscuit for each of her three boys in exchange for her help.

Captain Haynes, one of the Jayhawkers, tried to buy a biscuit from the Bug Smashers for a five-dollar gold piece. They refused his money—food was more valuable than gold. Haynes wept and said, "I have the best 160 acres in Knox County, Illinois, 100 stock hogs and 2000 bushels of old corn in a crib, and here I cannot get one biscuit for love or money."[7] He crawled under his camp blankets to spend another hungry night.

The Bug Smashers dried all the ox meat they could carry on their backs. They gave a liver from one of the animals to

Juliet. She set it aside for a few moments to finish the biscuits. When she returned to cook the liver for her children, it was gone—stolen by an unknown member of the camp.

The Bug Smashers also gave their 20 remaining oxen to the Briers, because the men could travel faster without the animals. The Bug Smashers set off by foot on December 28, 1849. Reverend Brier wrote, "When ready, they turned their faces away and reached out their hands. Not a word was said. As they receded my little group stood, eyes dimmed with tears and bitterly thought of the morrow."[8]

On December 29, 1849, the Briers followed the Jayhawkers across the snowy Panamint Mountains through Towne Pass, at the height of 5,000 feet (1,500 m). Reverend Brier carved his last name on a rock in the Panamints. It was common practice for westward-bound travelers to carve their name and date into rocks to show they'd passed. Modern historians use initials on these "rock registers" to track the routes of the pioneers.

The Bug Smashers were never heard from again. To this day, no one knows if any of the men escaped the desert. If they did, none of them ever wrote about their adventure as did so many of the other survivors. Some historians believe that they did escape, but were ambushed and killed on their way to the goldfields.

Years later, Indians reported finding the body of a white man lying in a pile of rocks in the desert. He had a broken leg and a bullet hole through his skull. His companions had been on foot and too weak to carry him, so there'd been nothing to do for the luckless man but to shoot him, rather than leave him to suffer and die from thirst alone in the desert.

One of the Jayhawkers, a man named Tom Shannon, buried $6,000 in gold coins that he'd carried with him from the Midwest. Although Shannon marked the spot where he'd buried his gold with rocks and brush, no one ever found the money that he'd hidden in the Panamint Mountains. Food and water were much more important than gold. Another man said, "Gold will not buy me a drink of water where there is none."[9]

It took only a few days for the Briers to find their way through the mountains trapping them in Death Valley. But they didn't know that 250 miles (400 km) of desert and mountains still lay between them and Los Angeles. For on the other side of the Panamints was another desert valley, then more mountains—the Argus and Slate Ranges. And the Mojave Desert and coastal mountains were obstacles still further ahead.

CHAPTER 8

THE ESCAPE PLAN

LIKE THE JAYHAWKERS and Briers before them, the Bennett party made their way into Death Valley. Unlike the Briers and the Jayhawkers, who'd abandoned their wagons at Forty Mile Canyon, the Bennetts, Arcans, and Wades found a route that allowed theirs to pass. They entered Death Valley with most of their possessions.

They traveled through a place today called Ash Meadows, a grassy clearing where cottonwood and ash trees grew, and wild grapes vined in tangled clusters. After filling water kegs and canteens at the spring in Ash Meadows, the group had pushed on toward Death Valley.

The only record we have of the Bennett and Arcan Christmas is that it was spent near a place that is today called Death Valley Junction. Their day was likely filled with long-ing thoughts of home. It took two days for the Bennetts and Arcans to cross the Funeral Mountains and labor down into Death Valley. By then, it was December 27, 1849.

Trailing behind the Bennetts and Arcans, the Wades cel-ebrated Christmas Day by themselves just outside of Death Valley. Mary Wade would not let the day pass without notice, however. "After having denied every demand for a few dain-ties she had kept hidden away in the grub box under the wagon seat, Mrs. Wade brought out the makings of an English plum pudding."[1]

Ash Meadows, Nevada, is 90 miles (145 km) northwest of Las Vegas.

During the passage across the plains from Missouri to Utah, Indians had stolen Mary Wade's cast-iron kettle. Determined to get it back, Mary hiked several miles in the dark the next night. She crawled under the side of an Indian tepee to retrieve the kettle. Mary Wade used it to prepare Christmas dinner for her family. That spunk and determination helped bring her family through the difficult and dangerous journey to Los Angeles.

One night as Manly trekked ahead of the families, he camped with the Jayhawkers. One of them said, "This must be the place where Lot's wife was turned into a pillar of salt," speaking of the story from the Old Testament of the Bible. "If a man were to die here he would never decay on account of the salt."[2] Large blocks of salt stood over salty sand. In some spots, salty water stood in shallow lakes and marshes. And a little creek running out of the mountains into Death Valley was as salty as the sea.

When Manly returned to the Bennett camp after overnighting with the Jayhawkers, he found that three of the oxen had been shot with arrows, possibly in retaliation for the theft of squashes from the Indians a few days earlier. Two of the oxen survived, but the third died, a serious loss to the party.

Like the forty-niners, the Indians in Death Valley also suffered from hunger in the winter after they depleted their stores of mesquite beans, pinyon nuts, and squashes. Manly had warned against stealing from the Indians. "I considered it bad policy to rob the Indians of any of their food, for they must be pretty smart people to live in this desolate country and find enough to keep them alive."[3]

As the new year began, Manly searched for an escape from Death Valley. For two weeks, the Bennett and Arcan families struggled along in his wake, trudging north and south along the length of Death Valley, looking for a way out. While they could have followed the Briers and Jayhawkers through Towne Pass, they were determined to find a route that the wagons could travel.

Occasionally a water spring was found, but little food. Only the children got bread, and often the water they found was too bitter or salty to drink. The hired drivers for the Bennetts and Arcans set off on their own to follow the Jayhawkers' tracks, abandoning the families they'd been employed to help.

Finally, the Bennett and Arcan families, along with Manly and Rogers, returned to the last place where they'd

located good water. They camped at a place in Death Valley now called Bennett's Long Camp. It had ample water and scrawny mesquite trees for shade, but little else. The Wade family also joined the Bennett party at the water hole. Eight single men with their own wagons still traveled with the three families.

The group held a meeting to devise a plan to escape from Death Valley, a plan they hoped could save all their lives. Manly and Rogers decided the best chance of getting out of Death Valley with the family wagons would be a southern route.

The mothers were desperately worried about their children. William Manly wrote about their situation. "We had a few small pieces of dry bread. This was kept for the children,

Bennett's Long Camp

giving them some now and then. Our only other food was in the flesh of the oxen, and when they failed to carry themselves along we must begin to starve. It began to look as if the chances of leaving our bones to bleach in the desert were the most prominent ones. One thing was certain, we must move on at once."[4]

Asabel Bennett had an idea. "I propose that we select two of our youngest, strongest men and ask them to take some food and go ahead on foot to seek a settlement. It surely will not take them more than ten days for the trip. When the oxen have rested a little at the spring, we can get out with our wagons and animals and be safe."[5]

Manly and Rogers volunteered to go for food and help. Preparations for the dangerous journey began. The weakest ox, one of Arcan's, was killed and its meat made into jerky. The men made several pairs of new rawhide moccasins for Manly and Rogers, while the women sewed leather knapsacks for them.

Manly and Rogers were poorly outfitted for such a dangerous trip. Their only food was 22 pounds (10 kg) of dried beef, and a few spoonfuls of rice and tea. Manly carried Bennett's seven-shooter rifle, and Rogers owned a double-barreled shotgun. They each had a knife, a tin cup, a small kettle, and a canteen made from two empty gunpowder cans tied together. The canteens held about a gallon of water. Manly wore his deerskin leggings from Wisconsin and a shirt. He carried half a blanket for warmth. Rogers owned a thin coat but had no blanket.

Jean Arcan gave Manly and Rogers $30. The other men collected all the money they had and also gave it to the boys (as Manly and Rogers were called), making a total of $60. The plan was for Manly and Rogers to reach civilization, purchase food and horses, and bring them back for the women and children to ride. Everyone offered advice to the two young men, although their wilderness experience exceeded that of the older men.

William Manly and John Rogers left the Bennett Camp in Death Valley in early January 1850. Manly wrote of that day, "Some turned away, too much affected to approach us, and others shook our hands with deep feeling, grasping them firmly and heartily, hoping we would be successful and be able to pilot them out of this dreary place into a better land. . . . [The Bennetts and Arcans] were the last to remain when the others turned away. . . . [Mrs. Bennett] asked God to bless us and bring food to her starving children."[6]

Manly went on. "We were so much affected that we could not speak, and silently turned away and took our course up the canyon. . . . After a while we looked back, and when they saw us turn around, all the hats and bonnets waved us a final parting."[7] But it would take much longer than the predicted ten days until the boys returned with help for those they left waiting in the desert camp.

CHAPTER 9

THE LONG WAIT

BECAUSE NEITHER THE BENNETTS nor the Arcans ever wrote about their time in Death Valley, one has to imagine their growing despair. As the days passed, food ran out although for once water was in plentiful supply. As the cattle died, their wretched flesh gave the camp barely enough meat to survive.

Every part of the cow was used. After burning the hair off the hide, it was crisped and eaten like pork rinds. Bones cooked in blood and water made up a distasteful soup. Men softened the ends of the horns in fire and chewed on them. Even the hooves were boiled for the few calories they might contain.

A Jayhawker named John Colton wrote about his experience with hunger at the age of sixteen. "For 52 days we hadn't a mouthful to eat, excepting when we would kill one of our oxen, or when one would die of starvation and thirst. As they had nothin' to eat but greasewood and cactus, they was tough eatin', but we eat up hide, blood, innards and all—couldn't afford to let a scrap go to waste. Sometimes we would find a big lizard and sometimes a little desert turtle to eat, but they was sceerce. We eat up all the snakes and ravens we could ketch."[1] This young man, about six feet (1.83 m) tall, left the desert weighing 63 pounds (28 kg). With thighs the size of arms, and knee joints like knots on a branch, he was a walking skeleton.

John Colton was photographed shortly after his Death Valley ordeal. He had lost 100 pounds (45.4 kg). Some joker was selling his picture as the only girl miner on the goldfields until John found out and stopped him.

Melissa Bennett told family members years later that she remembered being out of food except for the dry ox meat, which was "stringy and hard as a stick of wood."[2] When there was nothing else to eat, Sarah Bennett gave Melissa and Martha tallow candles to chew on before they went to bed without supper.

The Wades stayed only briefly at the camp with the Bennetts and Arcans. They'd said good-bye to Manly and Rogers along with the others when the boys set off looking for help. By January 15, 1850, Henry Wade was worried and impatient at waiting. His family was nearly out of food. Rationing cut each person's daily supply of flour to a tablespoon per meal, mixed into the thin beef soup.

Wade said to his wife, Mary, "If Mr. Manly and Mr. Rogers could go on foot for help, so can we."[3] He wasn't about to sit in camp and watch his family starve. Desperation gave him the courage he needed to try to find a way out of Death Valley for his family. Mr. Coverly, Henry Wade's original driver, had gone off on foot with the Arcan driver several days earlier. Wade hired one of the few remaining single men from the camp—a Frenchman named Schaub—to help his son Harry to scout and drive the wagons.

And so the Wades and their four children marched south looking for a way out of Death Valley. Wade concluded that the Old Spanish Trail must be in that direction. The mountains looked lower that way, and it seemed the logical thing to do. It was worth a try.

The men waiting in Bennett's Long Camp didn't believe Manly and Rogers would come back. After all, they had everyone's money, and it was a long and dangerous journey. Why should they return? "If those boys get out of this cussed hole, they are damned fools if they ever come back to help anybody," the men said of Manly and Rogers.[4]

Despite the Bennetts' reassurances about Manly's trustworthy character, the discouraged men began to leave camp on their own. "Our first duty is to save ourselves, and if fortunate, help others afterward," they declared.[5] Some of the men tried to catch up with Manly and Rogers, and some set off to trail the Wades.

Left at Bennett's Long Camp were Asabel and Sarah Bennett and their three children, George, Melissa, and Martha, and Jean and Abigail Arcan and Charlie, the youngest of all the children. Martha and Charlie both developed malnutrition; they had skinny arms and legs and bloated bellies. William Manly wrote that Martha looked "more like a big toad in shape, than like a child."[6]

All the food available was given to the children, but stringy beef is not enough to nourish a growing child. And there certainly wasn't any extra food for Mrs. Arcan, who was about four months pregnant. Most pioneer women didn't want to be a burden on the others, and they would seldom ask for extra food or water for themselves.

Loyal Cuff, George and Melissa's big white dog, was still with them, looking out for Indians, and ready to die for the family if he had to. Because food was scarce, Cuff hunted his own meager dinner in the sagebrush and sand. Small rodents, lizards, and broken bones from the dead oxen had to be enough for him. Only a few oxen still survived. The oxen were kept alive because they would be needed to carry supplies on the way out of the desert, so they were not slaughtered for food. Mr. Bennett and Mr. Arcan had promised to wait 18 days for Manly to return. However, when the boys hadn't returned by then, the parents decided that they would have to look for a way out of Death Valley on their own.

The two families had to try something. The children were starving before their eyes, and Martha had nearly died. They

Although survivors of the Death Valley forty-niners wrote hundreds of pages in letters, books, and diaries about their ordeal, no one ever mentioned that Abigail Arcan was pregnant. Perhaps no one except her husband knew. It wasn't until 1980 that the writers and researchers Leroy and Jean Johnson discovered an infant's grave beside Mr. Arcan's in Santa Cruz, California. Counting backward from the birth date shown on the baby girl's headstone, they realized that Mrs. Arcan was pregnant during most of the journey to California.[7]

In 1849, people didn't talk about women being "in the family way." Pregnancy was too personal and embarrassing for public conversation. Women whispered about childbirth only among themselves. Catherine Haun, a pioneer of the time, wrote about another woman in her diary, "Mrs. Lamore suddenly sickened and died, leaving her two little girls and grief-stricken husband. We halted a day to bury her and the infant that had lived but an hour." It's clear she died during childbirth, but the situation is referred to instead as a sudden illness.[8]

would try to follow the faint trail Manly and Rogers left on the hard desert floor. Although they never doubted that the young men would return if they could, the Bennetts now believed Manly and Rogers had perished in the desert while looking for help.

Sarah Bennett said, "We worked for a week fixing up for our almost hopeless journey. . . . We felt too bad to talk, and hardly spoke the whole day long. What could we do with these helpless children? I could see them in my mind suffering for want of food and water which could not be got for them. I saw them gasp and die."[9]

In despair, the parents sorted through their belongings in preparation for the risky journey. What to leave? What to take? The littlest children were too sick to walk. Their mothers made backpacks to hang on the oxen to hold Martha Bennett and Charlie Arcan. They would have to leave their wagons behind after all, because the remaining oxen were too few in number and far too weak to pull them any longer.

Finally, 26 days after Manly and Rogers had left, just one day before the two families planned to set off on their doomed journey, gunshots rang out through the clear desert air, shattering their mournful preparations.

CHAPTER 10

HORSE BONES CAMP

WHILE THE BENNETTS AND ARCANS waited for help in Death Valley, and the Wades traveled south looking for an escape from the desert, the Briers and the Jayhawkers continued westward. Shortly after leaving Death Valley, the Briers entered the Panamint Valley. There they found a deserted Indian village of willow wickiups nestled among the mesquite bushes. Only one old Indian woman remained. She scolded the group in her own language, worried at seeing the intruders. The ropes and bridles and horse bones littering the camp convinced the Briers and Jayhawkers that civilization was not far away.

But the village—which the Briers called Horse Bones Camp—wasn't a promise of civilization. For years it had served as a base for horse raids on the early Mexican settlements. The Indians and pioneers alike ate horses when other meat wasn't available. Some even preferred it to beef.

Frightened that the old woman's tribe would return to their village, the Briers left Horse Bones Camp and pushed on to another spot two miles away. There fresh water abounded, and the weary travelers rested for two days, gathering the strength to go on.

But only more desert loomed ahead, not civilization. Juliet said, "We grew more fearful of our provisions and watched each mouthful. Coffee and salt we had in plenty. The salt we picked up in great lumps before going over the last mountains. Our coffee was a wonderful help and had that given out, I know we should have died."[1]

New Year's Day 1850 went unnoticed as the Briers and Jayhawkers searched for a way out of the Panamint Valley. It seemed as desolate as Death Valley. "Sometimes we went south and again north not knowing whether we should ever get out of that death hole of sand and salt," wrote Juliet Brier.[2] "It was always the same—hunger, thirst and an awful silence."[3]

The party reached a swampy place, and the Brier's thirsty cattle rushed into the mud to drink and to eat the rough grass growing there. The men threw rocks and yelled at the animals, but nothing could make them come out of the muck. Instead, the cattle kept stepping into deeper mud until they became hopelessly trapped.

When Juliet walked into the mud to try to lead the oxen out she too, became stuck. Manly wrote about the scene that one of the Jayhawkers had described to him. "Her reverend husband sat on the hard ground at a safe distance, but didn't offer any help."[4]

Another Jayhawker named Stephens, helped Juliet and the cattle out of the gooey mess. Stephens said that if it had been "the Preacher" stuck in the mud, he would have left him there. No one knows why the Reverend Brier didn't help his wife.

Soon after that, the Briers spotted grizzly tracks, and the cattle stampeded when they smelled the bear. The oxen meant food and future money to the family, and some carried important supplies. They had to be recovered. A few of the oxen came back. Two men took their guns and went off to search for the others. A snowstorm cut the search short, and the missing

Panamint Valley

cattle were never found. The men returned with only a few wild cherries to show for their two days of searching.

Juliet Brier had been keeping a little flour owned by two men called Crumpton and Masterson. They were unhappy with her rationing it and asked Juliet to give it all back to them. "We shall have it while it lasts!" they declared.[5] The men did their own baking, then gave some dough to Juliet just before they left the mess on January 6.

Juliet said, "I made it into twenty-two little crackers and put them away for an emergency. That was our last bite of bread for six weeks. From then on my husband and I and the poor children and Loomis and Patrick lived on coffee and jerked beef."[6]

A few days later, the Briers overtook Crumpton and Masterson. The men were suffering agonizing starvation because they had eaten all their food. One of them, Juliet later wrote, had tears streaming down his cheeks. "I heard that man begging for even the entrails of a crow to eat."[7]

Black desert ravens hunched in low mesquite trees or flapped through the thin desert air, following the starving people and hoping for the chance to pick at their bones. The men hated the big, spooky birds and shot as many as they could.

Two Jayhawker stragglers caught up with the Briers and joined them. Father Fish was an elderly minister from Indiana who hoped to find enough gold to pay off his church's debts. He'd heard Reverend Brier preach back in Iowa, and that may have been his inspiration to go to California. Father Fish carried an expensive leather whip with him, wrapped around his waist. He hoped to trade it for food in Los Angeles.

Mr. Isham, the other man who joined the Brier mess, was Father Fish's driver, but the men's wagon was long gone.

The Panamint Range from Death Valley, California

Juliet's and Isham's families had known each other back in her childhood home of Vermont. Some of the survivors remembered Isham as a talented fiddler.

Juliet Brier recalled searching north and south for a way out of Panamint Valley, as escape became a race with death. "The valley ended in a canyon with great walls rising up as high as we could see. There seemed no way out, for it ended almost in a straight wall."[8] Terrible thirst made them miserable and threatened their lives. Salvation came in the form of a tiny water hole the Briers found. By digging into the sand, the family could scoop up about a pint of water an hour as it slowly seeped out.

It took more than a week to find a way out of Panamint Valley. Reverend Brier followed in the trail broken by the Jayhawkers, leading his family up the Slate Mountains, even though he needed two thick sticks to hold him up as he walked.

One day the men traveling with the Briers stayed behind to find some oxen that had strayed in search of water. When the lagging men started up the steep pass later that day, "Father Fish held onto the tail of one of the oxen for help in climbing the ridge. It was a hard climb, and just across the summit he reeled and fell and could go no further."[9] Everyone was so happy to finally escape Panamint Valley that they left Father Fish where he'd fallen and moved on. Juliet made coffee for him before she also left. It was common to leave stragglers behind and return for them later once water had been found.

The next morning Reverend Brier and another man went back with water for Father Fish, only to find him dead. The two men had to leave his body there with only a few bits of brush and stones piled about to shelter it from the desert sun. Reverend Brier likely said a prayer over Father Fish before he went on.

The Briers and the three men still traveling with them, Loomis St. John, Patrick, and Isham, continued following the Jayhawkers down the pass toward a huge, flat lake that today is called Searles Lake. It beckoned to them from afar, promising lifesaving water. But the undrinkable water was slimy and full of borax, and the exhausted group had to push on without relief from the extreme thirst.

Isham, driven crazy by his thirst, left the Briers and started crawling back to the lake, believing he could drink it after all. He fell as he crawled, never to rise again. When water was finally found, two men went back with some for Isham. But it was too late. Isham died just as his rescuers tried to pour water down his parched and swollen throat. The men found Isham's handprints in the sand. They calculated that he'd crawled nearly four miles trying to reach the poisonous water of Searle's Lake.

Reverend Brier later wrote, "The Jayhawks voted me Isham's watch and pocket book. His brother came on from Michigan in 1851 and found me in Marysville [north of Sacramento]. To him I delivered the property."[10]

The travelers had thrown away all their tools to lighten their loads. They had no way to dig a grave. Even if they had, the survivors were too weak for that heavy work. Father Fish and Isham were left as they fell, bones sounding a warning to those foolish enough to look for shortcuts through unknown, deadly deserts.

CHAPTER 11

DELIVERANCE

IT WAS NOW JANUARY 13, 1850. The Brier family had gone two days without water. They awoke the third morning without hope. The suffering was terrible. Juliet recalled those days as being the hardest of the long ordeal. "My husband tied little Kirk to his back and staggered ahead. His pitiful, delirious wails were worse to hear than the killing thirst. 'Oh, Father, where's the water?' he would cry. I staggered wearily behind with the other two boys and the oxen."[1]

Juliet went on. "The little fellows bore up bravely and hardly complained. They could hardly talk, so dry and swollen were their lips and tongues. John tried to cheer up his brother Kirk by telling him of the wonderful water we would find and all the good things we could get to eat."[2]

As Juliet Brier and her children trailed the men, she tended to weary Jayhawkers who'd given up and fallen behind. Despite her own worries about the welfare of her children, she always made time to help the dejected and desperate young men. Morale fell so low that men wrote farewell messages to their families back east, hoping that somehow relatives would receive the letters and know how they'd died.

One morning the Briers came upon two Germans from the Sand Walking Company who'd pushed far ahead. They cooked at a tiny fire.

"Any water?" asked Reverend Brier.[3]

"There's vasser," said one of the men, pointing the way to a muddy puddle.[4]

Juliet wrote, "The cattle rushed into it, churning up the mud, but we scooped it up and greedily gulped it down our burning swollen throats. Then I boiled coffee and found the pot half full of mud. It was awful stuff but it saved our lives."[5]

Sometimes the bladders of the slaughtered oxen were used to hold water. The canteens carried by the party were small. The large wooden water kegs had been abandoned along with the wagons.

Another day, when swollen tongues stuck out of sandpaper dry mouths, the Brier party believed the end was near. Only Juliet, praying behind a great rock, remained optimistic and determined to see her family survive. John Brier wrote, "My mother alone, rising from her prayers, was still confident. As she tried to reassure us, the last water hunter rushed into camp with news that he had found water."[6]

Legend says that Indians had pointed out the spring to a Jayhawker named Luther in exchange for his tattered shirt. That clear, cold spring bubbling from a great pile of rocks lies just north of today's desert town of Trona. Juliet Brier named it Providence Spring. Some of the Jayhawkers filled their canteens and hurried back along the trail to give the lifesaving water to comrades fallen behind. A man named Robinson died after drinking too much cold water all at once.

Columbus Brier had helped herd the family oxen on foot across much of the Nevada and California deserts. His father was either scouting ahead for water, or on some days, was too weak from his illness to manage the small herd. Following the others one day, Columbus took the wrong fork in a canyon. His mother feared that he'd been captured by Indians.

"But after a little searching he was found whistling behind his oxen and the error was soon corrected and the

Trona Pinnacles in Searles Lake, near Trona, California

anxiety released."[7] Juliet was relieved to find Columbus safe again, as well as the cattle. Only about a dozen cattle remained, and they would be needed to finance the family's future in Los Angeles.

Reverend Brier was quite ill by this time, so Juliet did most of the work. Each morning, she helped her husband to his feet and steadied him with two canes so he could walk. Juliet strapped the packs to the oxen every day and took them off at night. She built the campfire and cooked the food. She cared for the weakened Jayhawkers as well as her own children and husband.

There came a morning when Reverend Brier said he could go no further. "My husband laid down to die."[8] Juliet greatly feared the loss of her husband. "One more day of starvation would have ended his life. That would have been more than I could have borne."[9]

Food was still very scarce. Juliet tried grinding up acorns to make bread as the Indians did, but it was a failure. She didn't know that boiling the acorns leached out their bitterness. Only the tough jerked beef kept them going. Some days later, the men discovered a wild horse and shot it. The horse meat, fat and filled with needed calories and nutrients, saved their lives.

The survivors reported dreams of seeing clear rippling brooks, wading in beautiful ponds, and drinking water from cool, mossy wells. Visions of great loaves of bread, steaming beans and bacon, and delicious cakes filled their dreams. Then they'd wake up, and thirst and hunger tortured them even more than before.

Finally on February 4, 1850, deliverance came. Juliet Brier described it this way. "The sun was bright and the grass and flowers seemed like paradise after the awful sand and rocks of the desert. One of the men shot a hawk and another a rabbit, and we were preparing to feast on them. The wind blew the sound of lowing cattle toward us and we were in great wonder."[10]

Reverend Brier called to his wife, "Look Julie, no more starvation. We are here at last!"[11]

Asa Haynes, one of the Jayhawkers, wrote of the same scene, "Before me lay a little valley full of grass and trees and a beautiful stream of water running through it. The country was covered with fine fat cattle."[12] The gentle rolling hills were scattered with wild oats, clover, and oak and sycamore trees.

Juliet continued, "The Jayhawkers came rushing back with dilated eyes, saying they'd seen ten thousand head of cattle and wagon tracks, and believed we were near a farm. Oh, what excitement came over us! We came to where the men had killed a cow, when an old Spaniard and some Indian vaqueros came galloping up on fine horses. Our men expected trouble and held their guns ready."[13]

Juliet remembered how shocked the Spaniard was at their appearance. "We looked more like skeletons than human beings. Our clothes hung in tatters. My dress was in ribbons, and my shoes, hard baked, broken pieces of leather."[14]

Reverend Brier's trousers were ragged to the knees, his hair and beard grown long and tangled. His hat had lost its crown, and only its brim remained to shade his eyes. The three boys, also dressed in shredded clothing with feet wrapped in cowhide, stood silent and wide-eyed, staring at the unexpected newcomers.

The Spaniard and Indians didn't know English. But Patrick, one of the young men in the Brier mess, had served in the Mexican War and knew a little Spanish. Patrick pointed to Reverend Brier and said, *"Padre"*—priest.

The Spaniard understood that word. He took off his hat, bowed and said in a broken voice, *"Pobrecito Padre!"*—Poor little Father.[15]

John Brier remembered what happened next. "My brothers and myself were caught up by three swarthy vaqueros, who quickly carried us across the valley in spite of our squeals.[16]

Juliet wrote, "The Spaniard led us up to his house and the old lady there burst out crying when she saw our condition. They were very kind and cooked us a grand feast, killing the finest animal among their cattle in honor of the Padre."[17]

The rancher's wife and daughters were shocked at the family's appearance. They greeted Juliet and the children with tears and kisses. The generous Californios—a family by the name of del Valle—invited the Briers and the 32 Jayhawkers they traveled with to camp on a gentle hill near the ranch house. Señor del Valle sent squashes, beans, milk, and tortillas to feed the emaciated survivors. The Señora sent water and soap for washing tattered clothing and filthy skin.

"We fed like hungry animals," wrote John Brier.[18] After being so long without food, the travelers suffered severe stomach pain from the large meals. The Briers rolled on the ground with pain. A Dr. Irving from Los Angeles happened to visit the hacienda at this time, and gave them medicine to relieve the pain.

The del Valles were Californios, descendants of the early Spanish settlers of Mexico and California. Mexico (formerly called New Spain) had won its independence from Spain in 1821. Don del Valle, as he would have been addressed, presided over a huge tract, called the Rancho San Francisco. The ranchos were vast spreads of land in California that the governments of New Spain and Mexico had given to the Californios. The generous hospitality of the ranchos was a matter of pride, and Californio culture, a code of honor that said those in need were helped without question or recompense.

After resting a few days at the Rancho San Francisco, the Briers continued west to the San Fernando Mission. Their new friend, Dr. Irving, traveled with them. The Jayhawkers had already pressed on toward Los Angeles.

Fruit trees and gardens graced the mission grounds in the San Fernando Valley. John wrote about his memories of the mission. "We were permitted to sample the oranges and pomegranates, and in the evening were conducted through the old orchard. My mother asked Dr. Irving what the olives were."[19] The fruits and olives were new to the Briers.

Reverend Brier had managed to keep some of the money he'd brought with him from Iowa. The next morning, the Brier party purchased some animals so they wouldn't have to continue on foot to Los Angeles.

Loomis St. John selected a handsome gray mule. There was no saddle for the animal, and as soon as St. John mounted, the mule bucked and threw him to the ground. The young man rose, brushed off his clothes, and picked up his hat, ready for another try. The second time around, the mule allowed the inexperienced rider to remain in place.

John wrote, "A quiet bay pony was found for my mother. Two pillows served for a saddle. She was placed in position and I was lifted to a seat behind her. My younger brother was secured at the back of Dr. Irving by a silk handkerchief."[20]

John remembered the trip. "Twenty miles to Los Angeles. We had walked twice as far within twenty hours over waterless wastes of sand and stony mesa. This was a pleasure trip! We passed great herds of broad-horned cattle and sleek mares with foals. Halfway, we halted at a small hacienda and were greeted by a Señora, who invited us to enter for rest and refreshment. She fed us tortillas, milk and cheese. Beans and chili were in the tortillas."[21]

The group at last reached the end of their journey. "We halted in the evening on a hill overlooking Los Angeles. Chimes were calling to prayer [and] all was harmony," wrote John.[22]

Juliet had the final word. "It was like coming back from death into life again. It was a long, long weary walk, but thank God, he brought us out of it all."[23]

CHAPTER 12

OUT OF
DEATH VALLEY

AT THE BENNETT CAMP in Death Valley, Sarah Bennett called out joyously, "The boys have come! The boys have come!"[1] Manly and Rogers had fired shots to alert the others of their arrival. The boys rounded a huge boulder, guns held high and leading a mule. Bennett and Arcan caught the young men up in their arms. Sarah fell to the ground and held onto Manly's legs, crying with joy. Cuff barked and raced in excited circles.

Manly wrote, "No pen of man can describe the scene. They were so overjoyed they couldn't talk, but all eyes were moist and silence reigned for some time."[2] Everyone joined hands and walked back to the camp to share their stories. Abigail Arcan, who'd been resting under the shady wagon, joined in the greetings. Her failure to run out to greet Manly and Rogers is the only hint ever given of her pregnancy.

Bennett said, "I know you have found someplace, for you have a mule."[3]

"O, how glad I am," said Sarah, "you got back! We had given you up for lost, you were gone so long. All the others got discouraged waiting for you. They thought they had better go on and do their best while their cattle lasted."[4]

Everyone settled down to hear Manly tell about the long and arduous journey out of Death Valley. He and Rogers had crossed the endless peaks and valleys and deserts and had come to the del Valles' Rancho San Francisco, the same Californio ranch the Briers and Jayhawkers had earlier reached.

The kind lady at the ranch had pointed to her children and asked Manly with sign language, "How many children wait in the desert?"[5] Manly put his hand over his heart and held up four fingers to show there were four little ones. With tears in her eyes, she'd pressed oranges into his hands. Now Manly presented each child with one of the luscious fruits—the first they had ever seen. The oranges may have saved the children's lives by warding off the final ravages of scurvy.

Manly and Rogers continued telling the Bennetts and Arcans about their trip. They'd next purchased three horses and the mule, flour, beans, and meat. They'd rested only a day, then turned around and gone back the way they'd come, back into Death Valley toward Bennett's Long Camp.

The two men had been in a desperate rush to return with food for the families left starving in the desert. Manly and Rogers rode their new horses to exhaustion. In just a few days one died and the other two were too weak to go on. Manly wrote of the desolation the men felt as they abandoned the horses. Rogers had purchased a white mare and he was heart-broken. He wept as the horses whinnied in bewilderment and fear at being left alone in the desert. Just as bad, the women and children wouldn't have horses to ride out of Death Valley after all. They would have to walk or ride the oxen.

Manly had carefully buried part of the food he was carry-ing, planning to pick it up when the families were with them on the way out of Death Valley. The rest of the supplies had been packed onto the tough little one-eyed mule. She proved to be lively and sharp witted, and scampered nimbly over the steepest terrain.

Since Manly and Rogers knew the way back into Death Valley, it took only ten days for them to return to Bennett's Long Camp. Manly and Rogers had run into a Jayhawker who'd told them about Isham's death. Along the way, they'd turned aside for a few hours to look for Isham's body. When they found it, they buried him in the soft sand, then piled more of the sand into a mound to serve as a grave marker.

As the two young men were approaching Bennett's camp, Rogers had stumbled upon the body of a man called Culverwell—a retired sea captain. He lay on his back with arms outstretched, reaching toward his empty canteen. Manly feared that the families at Bennett's camp had fallen victim to the Indians, or else had died of thirst. They crept quietly toward the camp, prepared to find the worst. Then they fired a gun into the air knowing that if the people were still alive, they'd show themselves.

As Manly and Rogers finished their story, the two women remained silent as they realized how dangerous and difficult the trip ahead of them would be. They were terribly worried about their children. They were in poor health, all suffering from hunger and malnutrition. And, of course, Abigail Arcan was well into her pregnancy. Could the children survive the trip? Could the two mothers themselves live through it?

"It must be 250 miles yet to any part of California where we can live," Manly said.[6]

Then came the question, "Can we take our wagons?"[7]

Manly told them the bad news. "No, you will have to walk."[8]

In the end, the mere hope of relief from hunger and the desert was enough to rally up a little more courage. "We know

now just what we have to do and we'll do it. Can't we, Sally?" Bennett asked his wife, Sarah.[9]

The new provisions were unpacked, and the women prepared a hearty stew. Everyone talked about the escape plan long into the evening. Manly remembered that night well. "It was midnight before we could get them all satisfied with their knowledge of our experience. It was quite a treat to sleep again between good blankets, arranged by a woman's hand. It was much better resting than the curled up, cramped position we had slept in while away, with only the poor protection of the half blanket for both of us."[10]

The next day the adults hurried to finish the job of turning the canvas and wagon parts into harnesses and backpacks for five of the oxen. The women emptied the feathers out of their travel mattresses so they could use the strong cloth.

Martha and Charlie were far too ill to walk. Somehow they would have to ride on an ox. George and Melissa could ride together on another one, and each of the women would have one of her own to ride. "Such a thing as women riding on the backs of oxen had never been seen. Still, it occurred to us that it could be possible," wrote Manly.[11]

The oxen had never carried loads or people. They were only trained to pull heavy wagons—that was all they knew how to do. But the only choice was to try. The oxen fared a little better now after 26 days of rest and sufficient water. The bitter sagebrush and bits of grass growing near the spring had also strengthened them. They were in better shape than the people, who couldn't eat the vegetation and were only now regaining their strength.

The next afternoon Sarah Bennett and William Manly, who'd become close friends, sat in the shade of a wagon, chatting quietly together. As they sewed cloth harnesses, Sarah told Manly of dreams in which her children died one by one. She cried over the danger to them. How could the two families make it, if Manly and Rogers—the youngest and strongest of the men—had barely made it out and back?

Manly tried to calm Sarah's fears. "Try your best and we will make it as easy for you and the children as we can. . . . Courage and hope and the new provisions we have brought with us will help to build up your strength. . . . We will escape from this desert, unknown it seems, by the Lord himself."[12]

It was around February 10, 1850, that the preparations were completed. Bennett selected the ox named Old Crump to carry the children. Old Crump, with his brindled hide and bent horn, seemed the calmest and best tempered of all the oxen. Manly asked how the children could stay on without saddles.

Bennett said, "We have taken two strong hickory shirts, turned the sleeves inside, sewed up the necks, then sewed the two shirts together by the tail. When these are placed on the ox they will make two pockets for the youngest children. We think Melissa and George will be able to cling to his back with the help of a band around his belly."[13]

Martha and Charlie would be placed into the shirts facing outward. In this way, their mothers could feed the children as they marched next to the oxen. Manly wrote that it was sad to see Martha so helpless now when "just a few months before she'd scampered about camp as lively as a quail."[14] Even she was a little stronger, though, after a few meals of beans and flour mixed with the tough meat stew.

Manly and Rogers made themselves new moccasins from cowhide, for all of theirs had worn out on their long walk. The group could only carry the bare necessities. Each person wore all his clothing. One large cooking kettle, a tin cup for each person, eating utensils, water canteens, and food made up the supplies. Manly and Rogers also carried a rifle, a pistol, and a shovel. Everything else had to be left behind in the desert with the family wagons.

The next morning everyone was ready to go. The two women and four men rose early to prepare and load the oxen. Blankets and bedding served as saddles. It took several hours just to harness and load the oxen, because their skin hung loose and wrinkled around their thin bodies. They'd never had loads strapped to their backs, and fidgeted at the weight of the packs.

Of the original 16 oxen owned by the Bennetts and Arcans, five already had been eaten. The other 11 were to carry two five-gallon (19 l) wooden water kegs, the children, the women, and the supplies. Each adult carried a water canteen. Cuff would trot along with his family as usual. The mule, the most reliable animal, carried the valuable flour and beans.

Manly was very fond of his mule. "She could be trusted and would follow me like a dog. . . . She was as moral in her conduct as any one could be in a country where a man's morals are sometimes left as far east as the Missouri River."[15]

Abigail Arcan carried "fancy city finery" with her in the form of hats, ribbons, and bows. She wore a linen tablecloth that she had woven tied around her waist. Abigail was determined not to leave her beautiful things behind in the desert. "She got out her best hat and trimmed it up with extra ribbons, leaving some with quite long ends to stream out behind. She made one think of a fairy in gay and flying apparel."[16] Then she dressed little Charlie in his best Sunday suit for the trip.

Martha and Charlie were tucked into their shirt saddles on Old Crump. Then George and Melissa were lifted onto another ox, and told to hang onto the mattress-ticking band wrapped around its belly. Each of the women managed to climb onto an ox and cling precariously to its harness.

The group marched off in a line. Rogers went first leading an ox, then came Manly clutching the mule's harness. Bennett herded the loose oxen that didn't carry passengers. Arcan came next, leading Old Crump bearing Martha and Charlie, the smallest children. Melissa and George rode together on one ox. The two mothers came last, each balanced uncomfortably on the sharp spine of an ox.

The animals seemed content to plod along quietly on the soft sandy path for a few miles. Their feet were no longer sore after the long rest. Then a noisy commotion broke out. Manly described it this way. "The pack on one of the oxen near the lead got loose and turned over to one side. He tried to get away from it by jumping sidewise. Then he tried to kick it off, and really got his foot caught, making matters worse. He began a regular waltz and bawled at the top of his voice in terror." [17]

That frightened the other oxen. They all went crazy, the skinny animals bawling and bucking like wild horses. Sarah Bennett leaped off her ox. She shouted to Melissa and George to jump, and grabbed Martha from Old Crump. Jean Arcan grabbed Charlie from the opposite pocket and sat him on the ground while he tended to the rampaging animals.

Abigail Arcan managed to stay on her bucking-bronco ox. "She proved to be a good rider. She was tossed up and down and whirled about at a rate enough to make anyone dizzy. Her many fine ribbons flew out behind her like streamers from a masthead and the many fancy fixin's she had donned fluttered in the air in gayest mockery." [18] The ox finally succeeded in tossing Abigail to the ground, but she wasn't hurt.

Once it was clear that no one was hurt, the party broke out in laughter at the "impromptu circus which had suddenly

The oxen get frisky.

performed an act not on the program. The little mule stepped daintily to one side and looked on in amazement without disarranging any article of her load."[19] Of all the oxen, only Old Crump behaved himself.

It took hours to catch and calm the frightened oxen, repair the torn harnesses, and reload the packs. Soon after starting again, the Bennett party reached the place where Mr. Culverwell's body lay. Sarah gave Manly and Rogers a calico dress to wrap around the body as a shroud. The boys then buried Culverwell using the shovel they'd brought with them.

The two fathers left to search for water while the women cared for the children and made dinner. The group settled down for the night, after having traveled only four miles (6.4 km). They were determined to get farther the next day. They had to. Time and food were quickly running out.

CHAPTER 13

OX JUMP FALL

NEXT MORNING, the oxen kept their packs on and walked calmly along the trail. Although the animals behaved better that day, Abigail and Sarah decided to walk. Trying to ride the oxen proved more trouble than it was worth. Sarah Bennett trusted only Old Crump to carry her children, so all four children rode on the willing ox.

Martha and Charlie were popped into the carrying pockets made from shirts, one hanging on each side of the ox's shoulders. Melissa and George sat behind them, clinging to the strap around Old Crump's back.

The mothers took up positions alongside Old Crump to be near their unhappy children. Martha and Charlie fussed and cried at first. They were cramped and couldn't turn around or straighten out their legs. The ox's bony ribs continually jolted against their own thin bodies. The women tried to carry their children, but didn't have the strength.

The group fell into a daily routine. The four men ranged ahead of the women and children, looking for water, driving the oxen, and setting up camp when they found a good spot. The men did most of the cooking during the trip to conserve the women's strength. In the late afternoon, the two fathers, carrying water, would double back on the trail to meet their wives and children.

Asabel Bennett would lift his youngest daughter, Martha, from her pocket and carry her into camp. Jean Arcan still had his double-barreled gun with him. One day he threw it away, saying, "I have no use for you," so that he could carry his son Charlie whenever possible.[1]

Manly said, "When the women reached camp we had blankets already spread down for them, on which they cast themselves, so tired as to be nearly dead. They slept as they were. In the morning they sat up and looked around with uncombed hair, perfect pictures of dejection. Their swollen eyes and stiffened joints told how sadly unprepared they were to go forward."[2]

The Bennetts, the Arcans, William Manly, John Rogers, and Cuff the dog walking as the children ride old Crump

During the 26 days in Death Valley, waiting in fearful hunger, the women had lost much of their strength and endurance. But they always managed to go on, even though some nights they were too tired to eat after tramping all day through the desert. Despite her pregnancy, Abigail forced herself to keep up, asking no special favors, causing no delays.

It took only a few days to leave Death Valley, because Manly and Rogers now knew the way out. The families and two men stood atop a mountain, looking back at the deep, salt-encrusted floor of the valley they'd just left.

"Good bye, Death Valley," someone said.[3] Or maybe it was, "We have come out from the Shadows of the Valley of

Death."[4] Different sources credit the name to different people. According to Manly, his group named Death Valley as they left it. "We were the party which named it the saddest and most dreadful name that came to us."[5] Others said Juliet Brier named it, or an unknown Jayhawker. And other historians believe that members of a survey party named Death Valley years later when they mapped out the valley's length and breadth and depth.

Manly recorded a poem one of the Jayhawkers had composed while gazing across that vast wilderness:

> Yonder in mountains' gray beauty
>   wealth and fame decay,
> Yonder, the sands of the desert,
> Yonder, the salt of the sea,
> Yonder, a fiery furnace,
> Yonder, the bones of our friends,
> Yonder, the old and the young
>   lie scattered along the way.[6]

After the party left Death Valley, Manly and Rogers continued to serve as scouts, cattle drivers, and cooks. "A kettle of steaming soup, and blankets all spread out on which to rest, was the work Rogers and I did to prepare for the women. They sank down on the beds completely exhausted. The children cried some but were soon pacified and content to lie still. A good supper of hot soup made them feel much better."[7] It's almost certain the two families would not have survived if Manly and Rogers hadn't returned with food and knowledge of the way to Los Angeles.

The party had reached a dangerous point on their trip, a narrow ledge along a steep, sharp drop in the Panamint Mountains. It wasn't a tall cliff—only about 15 feet (4.6 m) high—but the trail along its edge wasn't wide enough for the children and oxen to walk safely. Manly had been thinking about this difficult spot for days and had worked out a plan to cross the ledge.

The four men went down to the foot of the cliff and moved rocks out of the way. Next, they shoveled all the sand they could collect at the bottom of the ledge. Manly stood below the cliff, while the other three men returned to the top. All the ropes they carried were tied together to make a single strong one. The men tied the rope tightly around the first ox's strong horns and led it to the edge of the precipice. They hoped the rope would hold the animal's head up and keep it from breaking its neck on the way down. The sand pile would protect the animals from injury when they landed.

"Now for it!" shouted Bennett, and the three men pushed the ox over the cliff.[8] It landed safely, sprawling in the sand with only a few small cuts. "Good enough!"[9] Bennett called.

One by one, the men pushed the oxen over the cliff. Rogers then smacked the little mule on her backside, and she leapt off and landed squarely on all four feet.

Next, Rogers joined Manly at the bottom of the ledge. The two fathers remained on the cliff with their families. They lowered the four children one by one down the cliff with the rope. The packs and supplies went next.

Then it was the women's turn. Manly wrote "Bennett and Arcan assisted their wives down along the little narrow ledge which we used in getting up, keeping their faces toward the rocky wall, and feeling carefully for every footstep."[10] And so the entire party of people and animals crossed the ledge in a couple of hours without injury. That place is now called "Ox Jump Fall."

The next morning the group passed the body of Father Fish. For the rest of her life Melissa Bennett remembered

Pushing the oxen down the precipice

seeing his body as she rode by on Old Crump. The men couldn't bury Father Fish because the ground was too hard for the shovel, and there was no sand or brush with which to cover him.

Two more days of difficult travel brought the party to the small stream where Manly had hidden the food on his way back into Death Valley. While the women and children lagged behind, the men made camp. They dug up the 40 pounds (18 kg) of wheat Manly had stowed, killed the weakest ox, and prepared a hearty meal. The extra fresh meat was dried into jerky over the smoldering campfire that night.

The people left bloody footprints on the hard, rocky ground as they walked. All the good shoes had long been worn out, and the rough moccasins only lasted a few days. Even the animals' feet bruised and then bled as they crossed the rough terrain. Rogers and Manly set about making new moccasins from the fresh rawhide for all the people and remaining oxen.

The party had been traveling only seven days. Although they did know that it would take fifteen more days to reach a settlement, the women doubted that they could go on. "Their appearance would quite strongly remind one of half-drowned hens. . . Hair snarled, eyes red, nose swollen. . . . They did not sleep well so much fatigued, for they said they lived over their hard days in dreams at night," said Manly.[11]

For their children's sakes though, the mothers gathered their courage and strength and went on. Manly helped by telling the two women about the beautiful streams, grass, flowers, and trees they would see at the Californio ranch.

Water continued in short supply. Manly told of the time he and Rogers had walked for 60 hours through the desert without water on their way out to get food for the families. The two men had been near death from thirst when they'd found a sheet of ice as thin as window glass, formed when dew froze over the low grass. That melted ice had kept Manly and Rogers alive as they struggled across the dry playa of China Lake searching for the next spring at Indian Wells.

The days went by. The men moved ahead as fast as they could, looking for water and herding the few remaining oxen. On some days the oxen had no water at all, and they grated their teeth in frustration and misery. When water was found, the men made dinner and camp for their families. The women plodded along several miles behind, with the four children riding Old Crump. The parents gave up most of their food and water to keep the children as comfortable as possible. Martha and Charlie suffered painfully cramped legs from riding in the carrying packs.

Little Charlie broke out with a terrible rash all over his body, so red that it looked like a burn. Without medicine or sufficient water, little could be done for him. He may have been allergic to Old Crump. He'd been in close contact with the ox for days, with only a thin shirt between his delicate skin and the animal's tough hide. All his mother, Abigail, could do was to sprinkle clean sand over the rash and hope it helped. Charlie cried much of the time from the pain and itching of the rash.

One night in late February it began to rain. As everyone huddled together for warmth under the thin blankets, the rain turned to snow. By the time morning came, two inches (5 cm) of snow had fallen. At least there was enough water to drink that day. Hungry and cold, wet and miserable, the party struggled to keep enough hope alive to go on.

All food ran out except the "beef-on-the-hoof" provided by the sick, weak oxen. Every few days the weakest one was killed for food. The families still hoped to have a few animals left alive to sell when they reached Los Angeles. They were

China Lake, California

destitute, with hardly a penny among them and very little to trade.

Arcan carried Charlie when he could, as it helped relieve his rash to be off the ox. This left the pocket saddlebag unbalanced, so Bennett had to also carry his youngest child, Martha. Manly and Rogers continued to move far ahead of the others, herding the few remaining oxen with them.

The rough rawhide moccasins wore out again, and bare feet grew blistered and bloody. With tender hooves, the oxen picked their way slowly and carefully between the hard, jagged rocks. Bones of horses and cattle littered the trail, proving that other animals had died between water holes. Only the thought of good food, cool water, and an eventual end to the desolate landscape kept everyone going.

One morning, things began to look better. Manly shot a stray fat cow he found. Fresh meat and rawhide for new moccasins cheered everyone up considerably. Finding a cow to eat meant that they could keep their own animals alive for a few more days. And the cow meant that civilization must lie not far ahead.

Manly wrote about those last days on the trail. "Arcan's boy Charlie still suffered from his bogus measles or whatever his disorder might be. Bennett's little Martha grew more quiet and improved considerably in health, though still unable to walk. George and Melissa seemed to bear up well and loved to get off Old Crump and walk in places where the trail was smooth and level." [12]

Manly estimated that about five days of travel across the Mojave Desert remained. Everyone felt stronger after eating the fresh meat. The mule required little water and never strayed far. Old Crump "bore the same four children every day, faithfully, carefully, with never a stumble or fall, as though fully aware of the precious nature of his burden." [13]

One night Manly killed another wild cow he found while scouting ahead with his mule. Then he got lost in the dark and couldn't find his way back to camp with the fresh beef. The Bennett's dog, Cuff, found Manly and led him the ten miles (16 km) back to camp, possibly saving his life.

Not many dogs had traveled successfully across the country. Often families had to abandon their dogs because their feet became too sore to walk, and they couldn't be carried in the wagons. Manly wrote, "Cuff did not propose to be left behind to starve, and crippled along after us. He proved as tough as the best of us. Bennett and I had trained him as a

The Mojave Desert

hunting dog in the East, and he was very knowing and handy in every particular."[14] Cuff stood watch and gave warning of anything unusual. He was the only Sand Walker dog known to have survived.

The nights became colder as the group slowly climbed yet another mountain range. Snow covered the peaks. Yet even though it was only late February, the days were often very warm. Sometimes the ragged party followed the broken trail of the Jayhawkers, and other times they forged their own. Once they had to lurch through a snowfield many miles wide and three feet deep. Then they crossed the San Gabriel Mountains—the final barrier between them and Los Angeles.

The Bennett-Arcan party walked through the land on which Edwards Air Force Base is built. Today the space shuttles land there.

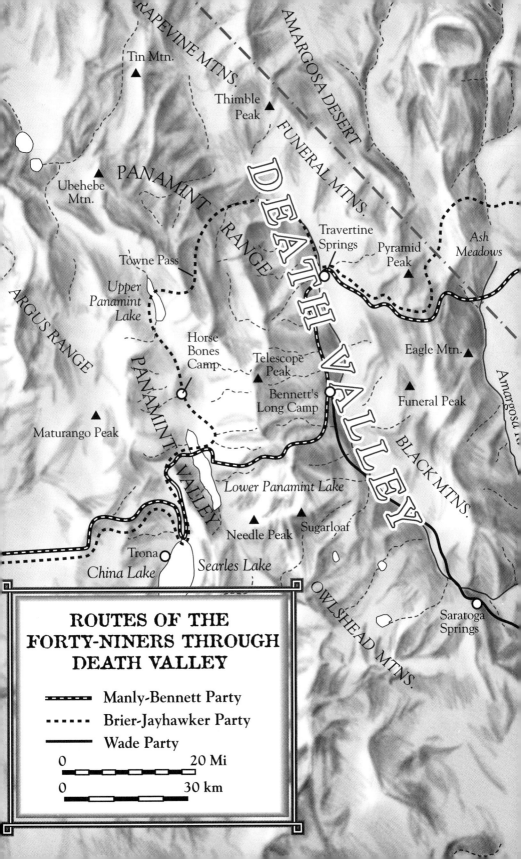

ROUTES OF THE
FORTY-NINERS THROUGH
DEATH VALLEY

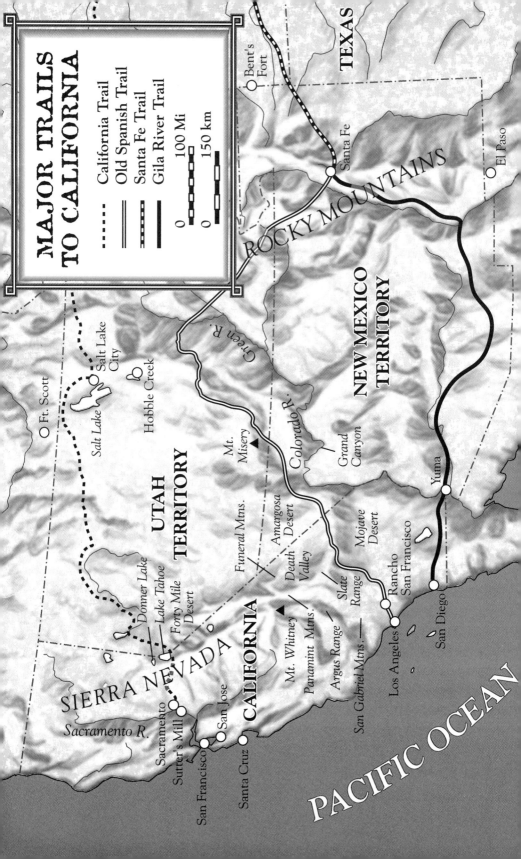

MAJOR TRAILS TO CALIFORNIA

- · · · · · · California Trail
- ———— Old Spanish Trail
- - - - - - Santa Fe Trail
- ——— Gila River Trail

0 — 100 Mi

0 — 150 km

TEXAS

Bent's Fort

Santa Fe

El Paso

ROCKY MOUNTAINS

NEW MEXICO TERRITORY

Green R.

Ft. Scott

Salt Lake City

Hobble Creek

Salt Lake

UTAH TERRITORY

Mt. Misery

Colorado R.

Grand Canyon

Yuma

Funeral Mtns.

Amargosa Desert

Death Valley

Mojave Desert

Rancho San Francisco

Donner Lake

Lake Tahoe

Forty Mile Desert

Slate Range

Los Angeles

San Diego

SIERRA NEVADA

Mt. Whitney

Panamint Mtns.

Argus Range

San Gabriel Mtns.

CALIFORNIA

Sacramento

Sutter's Mill

Sacramento R.

San Jose

San Francisco

Santa Cruz

PACIFIC OCEAN

CHAPTER 14

RETURN TO CIVILIZATION

The Wades

Meanwhile, the Wades and their driver, Schaub, were making their own way south, out of Death Valley. Henry Wade consolidated the family belongings into one wagon and left the other behind. A horse named Pet—fitted with English saddle—traveled with the Wades as they left Bennett's Long Camp on January 15, 1850. Their cow, Rosie, also followed along, tied to the tailgate of their wagon.

Although the Wades were running low on food, they couldn't slaughter their remaining four oxen or the cow. The oxen were needed to pull the wagon, and Rosie produced milk for the children. The animals fared better than the people did, eating sagebrush and other vegetation along the way.

But the four children and three adults suffered terribly from hunger. At one point, the only thing keeping them alive was half a cup of milk each day. If Rosie didn't get sufficient water to produce enough milk, only the youngest children, Almira and Richard, got any.

One of the Sand Walkers, named Culverwell, caught up to the Wade wagon. He was near death from thirst and exhaustion. Henry Wade refused him help, believing that his supplies were barely enough for his own family. Culverwell left the Wades to head back to Bennett's Long Camp, where he knew water could be found. He died before he could reach the camp. It was his body that Manly and Rogers discovered when they returned to the Bennett camp with the supplies and mule. Although they feared Culverwell had been killed by Indians, thirst and hunger caused his death.

The Wades could carry a lot of water with them. Henry Wade had purchased large metal milk cans from a Mormon dairy farmer near Salt Lake City at the beginning of the trip. Unlike the wooden water kegs carried by the others, water couldn't leak or evaporate from the metal containers.

But a big family traveling through the desert with animals needs a lot of water. By the end of the third day, the water carried by the Wades in their milk cans and canteens was gone. When the oxen were unhitched at the dry camp that night, the thirsty animals stampeded back toward the Bennett camp, remembering the plentiful water there. It took Wade, his son Harry, and the hired hand, Schaub, all night to catch the cattle and bring them back.

The Wade mess was in a dangerous position, out of water and food, and unsure if they were even going in the right direction. At sunset, while Almira sat on the wagon seat, she watched two desert ravens swoop down from the sky and disappear behind a nearby sand dune. Almira may have remembered the advice given to wagon trainers, "Watch the animals. Deer go toward water at mid-day. Birds fly to water at night."[1]

Almira jumped down from the wagon and climbed the sand dune only 300 yards (275 m) from the wagons. Beyond it lay a clear lake of fresh water that saved their lives. Although the Wades were tempted to rest at the spring, they were growing weaker each day. Starvation threatened the entire family. They filled up the milk cans and canteens with water and pushed on.

The Wades left Death Valley and entered the Mojave Desert, a place with even less water. Henry Wade and Schaub scouted ahead for water and grass for the oxen, while young Harry drove the wagon that carried his mother, sister, and two brothers. When the men found water, they made a fire and sent up smoke signals to guide the wagon to them. On some days, they didn't find water and had to make do with a dry camp. And there still was no food for the people.

A 50-mile (81-km) "journada"—a journey without water—separated Saratoga Springs and the Mojave River. For several more days the Wade party struggled across the terrible barren desert to reach the Mojave River. Thirst finally satisfied, water kegs filled once more, the Wades followed hoofprints of horses along the wide path beside the river bank. They had reached the Old Spanish Trail at last.

On January 29, 1850, the Wades caught up to prospectors who told them that civilization was only 60 miles (96 km) away. The miners sold the family a bucket of biscuit flour. Because the Wades still had their wagon, they had money and goods to trade.

Grass by the side of the river fed the weakened oxen. The family hurried on, encouraged by the food and water, and the knowledge they were headed the right way. West of San

Almira Wade found the water, now called Saratoga Springs, that marks the extreme southern end of Death Valley. It's now known that the Amargosa River surfaces from its underground course beneath the desert at Saratoga Springs.

Saratoga Springs, California

Bernardino, some cattlemen took the weary travelers into their camp and fed them. For the first time Almira tasted flour tortillas fried in fat. "It was the best meal I ever ate in my life," she later remembered.[2]

It began to rain, the first downfall they'd seen since leaving Salt Lake City. Wet and weary but hopeful, the Wades kept going west along the Old Spanish Trail. On February 10, 1850, nearly a month ahead of the Bennetts and Arcans, and a week after the Briers, the Wades reached the Californio ranch near Los Angeles called San Jose Rancho. Their difficult, long journey from Missouri was finished.

No one who'd met the Wades on the journey from Salt Lake City knew what had happened to them after they left the Bennett camp. For many years, rumors flew among the surviving lost forty-niners that the Wades had perished trying to escape the desolation of Death Valley.

In fact, of the 27 wagons that took the nonexistent short-cut, only the Wades made their way out of Death Valley with their wagon and personal belongings. Though they'd passed wagons abandoned by the Jayhawkers and Briers, the Wades somehow always managed to find a trail their wagon could traverse. It wasn't until 1894 that a letter published in the *San Jose Pioneer* gave Almira Wade's account of their escape.[3]

If the lost forty-niners had known that the way out of Death Valley was so close, they would have been spared much hardship and suffering. L. Dow Stephens, one of the Sand Walkers, later wrote, "Wade had taken his family and struck south down that valley, and struck the Old Spanish Trail at the Mojave, which is the way we all ought to have went."[4]

The Bennett Party

Two days from civilization, the weary Bennett party camped under a huge oak tree. A stream gurgled nearby, and for the first time in months, the oxen had enough to eat and drink. Relaxing in the shade, they contentedly chewed their cuds.

The people washed themselves and their clothes as best they could and rested up for their final effort. The women hoped to get new dresses soon—two apiece, they said—long enough to cover their ankles, unlike the short tattered rags they now wore.

The next day the tired party relaxed in a green meadow full of cattle. Frisky calves raced each other in circles, then found their mothers to feed. Water merrily chortled its way through the grass and over stones. The adults began to think about their next steps—rest awhile in Los Angeles, or hurry north to the gold mines?

It had taken four months from leaving the trail to look for the impossible cutoff on November 4, 1849, to reach civilization on March 7, 1850—four agonizing months spent lost in the wilderness, struggling to stay alive. Everyone agreed they would never again try a shortcut.

The shabby party crossed the last ridge and reached the del Valle family at the Rancho San Francisco 17 days after leaving Death Valley. Señora del Valle came to greet the Bennett party with her child clinging to her skirt. *"Mucha pobre,"* she said, meaning that the Bennett and Arcan children were very poor. *"Flaco, flaco,"* she said, of the oxen—thin, thin.[5] She remembered Manly and pulled an orange out of her pocket. "Did you give the oranges to the children in the desert?" she asked by hand signals.[6] She smiled when he said yes. Then the kind Señora gave more oranges to the four children.

The ranch hands rode up on fine horses. They wore cowhide chaps on their legs, wide-rimmed hats, and boots with silver spurs. Braided lariats coiled in tight circles around the saddle pommels. Manly watched the cowboys ride through the cattle, managing the animals with horses and ropes. He'd never seen anything in the Midwest like those Californio cowboys. They roped a young calf and butchered it for lunch along with fresh milk, still warm from a cow. This was the first milk the four children had tasted for months.

After Jean Arcan told the Californios that he was a Catholic (although he was a Protestant), the Arcans and Bennetts were invited to spend the night at the ranch house. The Californios had also believed the Reverend Brier to be a Catholic. Maybe the forty-niners believed that the ranchers would be more friendly to those of their own religion.

The ranch folk gave the Bennetts and Arcans an abundance of delicious food for dinner, some of it new to them—tortillas, beans seasoned with peppers, cooked squash, and hot chili with meat. At the end of the night, evening prayers were held. Then the children were wished *"buenos noches"* and tucked into soft beds.[7]

The del Valles refused all payment from the groups of Sand Walkers they had helped—first the Brier family and about 32 Jayhawkers, then the Bennetts and Arcans, Manly, and Rogers.

The party broke up the next morning. The Arcans didn't plan to go to Los Angeles. Instead, they headed directly to the Pacific Coast. Before Arcan left, he gave a gold ring to Manly and a silver watch to Rogers in thanks for saving his family. "I can never repay you," he told the men. "For I owe you a debt beyond compensation. You saved our lives, and have done it when you knew you could get nothing for it."[8]

The Arcans traded their last two oxen for supplies. Then, with tearful eyes and emotion-choked voices, they said good-bye to the Bennetts and the two boys—Manly and Rogers. Abigail Arcan rode a loaned horse, holding Charlie in her arms. The Arcans set off with a local guide. Other than the clothes they wore, their only remaining possessions were Abigail's lace tablecloth, Jean's telescope, and a few worn blankets.

The rest of the party—the Bennett family, Manly, and Rogers—pushed on with three oxen, the mule, and Cuff. The del Valle family called, *"Adios,"*[9] as the children were loaded onto Old Crump. Well-fed and happy that their journey was nearly over, the group began marching the last 20 miles (32 km) to Los Angeles.

It had been nearly a year since the Bennetts and Manly had left Wisconsin. Everyone was grateful to be nearly done

with their journey, but they had mixed feelings about the future. They were ragged and destitute, without a dollar among them. How could they make new lives for themselves in California?

The Bennetts, Manly, and Rogers approached Los Angeles looking for a place to camp. The town was largely Spanish. There were a few wagons in its streets. Manly described what he saw. "The houses were only one story high, and seemed built of mud of a gray color, the roof flat."[10] Some of the inhabitants lived in tents along the crooked, dirt lanes.

Manly wrote, "Our strange appearance attracted the attention of children, and they kept coming out of the houses

Los Angeles,
California,
circa 1850

to see the curious little train, with Old Crump carrying the children, and our poor selves following along, dirty and ragged. Mrs. Bennett's dress hardly reached below her knees and her skirts were fringed about the bottom."[11] Sarah's shabby dress made her ugly rawhide moccasins all the more noticeable.

As the tattered party walked among the tents, two men ran out. "My God, it's Bennett!" one of them shouted.[12] They were Judge Henry Skinner and Mr. Moody, Wisconsin neighbors who had traveled with the Bennetts across the plains to Salt Lake City. From there, they'd started out on the same route to Los Angeles. But the Bennetts had taken the supposed shortcut, while their friends had gone along with Captain Hunt on the Old Spanish Trail.

The Moodys and Skinners had been waiting more than six weeks in Los Angeles for the Bennetts, not knowing if they'd lived or died in the desert. Judge Skinner and Moody had vowed to go into the desert themselves to look for the Bennetts; now they didn't have to make the risky trip.

Asabel and Sarah Bennett and their three children were invited into Moody's tent, where Mrs. Moody gave them soap and water, new clothes, and combs for their tangled hair. Bennett got a much-needed haircut and shave. The family emerged two hours later clean, refreshed, and happy to have reached this point.

Manly and Rogers went on with the oxen and mule to set up camp under a willow tree, returning to the family tents for dinner. It took until midnight to tell the story of the four-month-long desert crossing to the Skinner and Moody families.

The next morning, Bennett traded his rifle for a small wagon and harnesses for their remaining pair of oxen. His friends generously replenished his food and supplies. Then the Bennetts left Los Angeles with the Moodys and Skinners to head north toward the goldfields. Rogers needed work but hadn't been able to find any in Los Angeles, so the three families hired him to help with the teams.

Manly said a final tearful good-bye to his friends and companions. Taking the little mule that Bennett and Arcan had given to him, he went to the Los Angeles boardinghouse where he had just found work—a boardinghouse owned by Reverend Brier!

CHAPTER 15

THE FAMILIES AFTER DEATH VALLEY

The Briers

When they reached Los Angeles, the Briers stayed with Dr. Irving, the man who'd traveled with them from the Rancho San Francisco. After regaining his health, Reverend Brier preached. His audience collected $10 for the preacher and his family—a tidy sum of money in those days.

Reverend Brier next looked for business opportunities. He formed a partnership with one of the men on the wagon train who'd continued on the Old Spanish Trail with Captain Hunt. Together they bought a boardinghouse, with Reverend Brier selling some of his remaining oxen to pay for his half. By mid-March 1850, the boardinghouse was in operation, full of people on their way to the goldfields of central and northern California. As usual, Juliet did most of the work—the cooking, washing, and cleaning for the guests, as well as for her family.

John wrote of the Brier boardinghouse, "The house was equipped with a bakery, a barber shop, and a blacksmith shop. My father also had personal charge of a fine old vineyard."[1]

Although Reverend Brier paid for the boardinghouse, he was a "squatter" on the vineyard land. He declared, "I am an American, and this land is part of the public domain."[2] Reverend Brier felt free to take over property that likely had been owned by a Californio. (Mexico lost California to the United States in the Mexican War [1846–1848], and California would become the 31st state in September 1850.)

Columbus and John attended a private school in the house of one of the American settlers. While Juliet may have given her children lessons during the trip from Iowa to Utah, the journey from Salt Lake City to Los Angeles had been too difficult to continue with their studies. "I learned how much I had forgotten," John wrote.[3]

Los Angeles was entirely different from any place they had known. Fandangos and fiestas, tile-roofed adobe houses, and bullfights in the plaza told of its Mexican heritage. The temblors, or earthquakes, were Californian, as were the many gambling houses.

The Briers prospered in California. By the middle of the year, they had saved enough money to leave Los Angeles. The family moved to northern California, where three daughters were born. Juliet's heirloom silverware was found in the desert twelve years later by a survey party and returned to her.

Reverend Brier saw to it that his sons got a good education, as he had advised in his Christmas Eve lecture in 1849. The boys made their parents proud of them. Columbus became a professor of mathematics and science at a private college near San Francisco. Kirk, the youngest Brier boy, was also a teacher and the principal of Sacramento High School. Kirk was only forty-three when he died. Family members believed that his early death was due to the starvation and thirst he'd suffered on the journey.

John, the middle boy, became a prominent minister like his father. When he grew up, he wrote about the lost forty-niners. Later historians thought he was too young to have remembered much about the journey, and that what he wrote were memories of stories his parents told him. Still, his recollection of the events added another dimension to the tales.

Memories of the trip through the deserts of Nevada and California remained with the survivors for the rest of their lives. Thirty years after the ordeal, Reverend Brier wrote, "I go back in my mind over the whole trip about 200 times per annum. Even at this distant day I can describe every mile of the way with every camp and every incident of the journey."[4]

Reverend Brier returned to Death Valley several times and once, in 1873, to the Panamint Mountains as a guide for some miners. During one of his trips back, Reverend Brier said, "As we struck our old trail it seemed to me that it was but yesterday when we passed. The journey was one of intense interest and deep solemnity. At many a point where we suffered most I went alone into the rocks and sage and wept and thanked God for our deliverance."[5]

A loyal Republican, Reverend Brier campaigned in California on behalf of Presidents Lincoln, Grant, and Garfield. Occasionally, he gave speeches about his Death Valley adventures around the state for extra income. Reverend Brier lectured in Los Angeles when he was seventy-three and captivated the audience with the details of his long-ago ordeal. Reverend and Mrs. Brier lived with their son, John, most of their later life.

The Briers kept in touch with the Jayhawkers through the years. Reverend and Juliet Brier were often invited to attend the Jayhawker reunions, celebrated each year on February 4, the date that the Briers and Jayhawkers reached the Rancho San Francisco. Although Reverend Brier didn't attend the reunions, Juliet did. In fact, she hosted a Jayhawker reunion in 1902, when she was eighty-eight years old! In 1911, three of the five surviving Death Valley forty-niners held a reunion at Mrs. Brier's home when she was ninety-seven.

The Death Valley forty-niners were divided in their opinions of Reverend Brier. Manly and some of the Jayhawkers who wrote about their journey expressed disgust at what they viewed as his laziness and dependence on his wife to perform work he should have done.

But not everyone felt the same way. Some recognized that Reverend Brier's illness and huge weight loss had weakened him. One of the Jayhawkers wrote, "No matter what the difficulties were or how panic stricken the others all were, [Brier] was uniformly unruffled and calm. He was an honest and kind-hearted man."[6] Mrs. Brier always vigorously defended her husband, saying that he had been severely debilitated by dysentery and near starvation.

However, all the Jayhawkers held Mrs. Brier in high regard. They thought her the strongest and bravest member of the wagon train. The young Jayhawker John Colton said, "Her devotion and courage, her unfailing kindness to the remaining members of the party inspired them with the greatest love and affection."[7]

Juliet Brier wrote two accounts of the journey before she died in 1913 at age 99, in Lodi, California. She had traveled across the country in an ox-drawn wagon, and lived long enough to see automobiles and airplanes. Juliet outlived all but four of the young Jayhawkers who had traveled through Death Valley with the Briers.

The Bennetts

The Bennetts and their children all regained their health—even Martha, who'd been so close to death. They mined for gold near the Merced River in central California. Later, they moved to Georgetown in northern California, then to Monterey on the coast. By 1854 another son and daughter were born. They named the boy John Rogers in honor of the man who'd helped to save the family.

Sarah Bennett died of tuberculosis in a San Jose hospital in 1857. Manly rushed to his friend's bedside, arriving barely in time to say good-bye to her. After his wife's death, Bennett left his youngest child, a toddler named Ella, with a family near San Jose. He moved to Utah with his four older children and married a Mormon woman. Bennett decided that he didn't care for Mormon life after all, and he left his second wife and moved to Los Angeles.

Bennett drifted aimlessly through the West for the rest of his life, prospecting for gold and silver. Some thought the terrible experience of crossing the desert affected his mind. He often wasn't on good terms with his children. A Jayhawker wrote that some of the men who crossed the desert "never did get entirely in their right minds again."[8]

The Arcans

Jean Arcan and his family reached the ocean port of San Pedro, where he traded his telescope—worth $10—for sail passage for his family to Santa Cruz, south of San Francisco, then a tiny seaside village. Only Abigail's tablecloth remained from all their household goods.

Abigail Arcan didn't join her husband when he left Santa Cruz to prospect for gold with Bennett. She told him, "You can go to the mines if you want to. I have seen all the God-forsaken country I am going to see, and I'm going to stay right here as long as I live."[9]

She remained in Santa Cruz with little Charlie, to await the delivery of a baby girl, born on July 1, 1850. The infant, named Julia, after Juliet Brier, lived for only 19 days. Because Abigail suffered from near-starvation and thirst for much of her pregnancy, it's likely her baby was born small and weak. Baby Julia Arcan was the first person to be buried in the Santa Cruz cemetery. She's been called the littlest victim of Death Valley. This poem is carved on her small headstone:

> *A little time on earth she spent*
> *'Till God for her his angel sent*
> *And then on time she closed her eyes*
> *To wake in glory in the skies.*[10]

Jean Arcan found gold and returned to Santa Cruz, where he purchased land, and was said to be a kind and friendly man. He and Abigail were respected citizens. Abigail had two other daughters later and again named one of them Julia, after Juliet Brier. She gave her treasured tablecloth, carried through Death Valley and across the Mojave Desert, to her daughter-in-law, Charlie's wife.

The Wades

After spending a short time regaining their health in Los Angeles, the Wades went to the Mariposa gold mines near Yosemite. They found enough gold there to finance a move to Alviso, a small town near San Jose where they lived for the rest of their lives. Mary Wade had a baby girl she named Mary Ann, born in January 1851, less than a year after they'd escaped from the desert. The baby was born under an oak tree in the same covered wagon that had carried the Wades out of Death Valley. Wade grandchildren used the old wagon as a playhouse for years.

Henry Wade and his son Harry went into the teaming business, hauling freight by horse-drawn wagons. They opened a hotel called The American House but it later burned down. Wade held public office as justice of the peace. In 1893 he died from an accidental gunshot wound, and Mary died four years later.

When Almira grew up and married, she kept books for the family business. Her elder brother Charles owned strawberry and raspberry fields, as well as a dairy. The youngest son, Richard, also went into the transport business, driving wagons and stagecoaches.

In 1957, Historical Landmark No. 622 was erected in Death Valley by the California State Park Commission to mark the route Henry Wade took. Descendants of Henry and Mary Wade officiated at the unveiling of the monument, which reads:[11]

> *After being in Death Valley with the ill-fated 1849 caravan, Henry Wade found this exit route for his ox-drawn wagon, thereby saving his life and those of his wife and children. At this point the Wade Party came upon the known Spanish Trail to Cajon Pass.*

Manly and Rogers

While the Bennetts rested with the Moody and Skinner families for a few days, William Manly and John Rogers had looked for work in Los Angeles. Manly wrote, "We came to a boardinghouse and went in and sat down in the empty room. Soon a man came in, better dressed than ourselves, and much to our surprise, it was one of the old Death Valley travelers, the Reverend Brier, whom I last saw in his lone camp in the desert, discoursing to his young sons on the benefits of an early education."[12]

Reverend Brier told them he could afford to hire only one man, who could drive oxen. Manly was the more experienced driver, so he got the job. Rogers hired on with the Bennetts, and headed north with them to the gold mines.

Manly's duties at the Brier boardinghouse included hauling water by oxcart and pulling weeds in the vineyard. His wages were $50 a month, including room and board. However, he stayed only two weeks. Manly said, "Grub disappeared pretty fast at my corner of the table for my appetite began to be ravenous."[13] While he certainly enjoyed Juliet Brier's cooking, perhaps he didn't like his bed, which was atop a pile of old rags and blankets in a storeroom!

With the money he'd earned at the Brier boardinghouse, he started up the coast of California with a pack full of meat and crackers and only his faithful mule for company. Manly also purchased a "Spanish blanket having a hole in the center through which to put the head and wear as a garment"[14] It was the first poncho he'd ever seen.

As Manly traveled, he overnighted at the Spanish missions, conveniently spaced a day's travel apart. He enjoyed the hospitality at Santa Barbara, San Luis Obispo, San Juan Capistrano, and other missions. He marveled at his first sight of the ocean. "The seashore was the grandest sight in the world to me, for I had never before seen the ocean. What a wide piece of water it was! Here the waves kept coming, one after another, with as much regularity as the slow strokes of a clock."[15]

On his way north, Manly ran into John Rogers, who told him that Bennett and Moody were camping nearby. Manly hurried to rejoin his old friend, Asabel Bennett. Just south of San Francisco, Manly experienced his first earthquake. "I felt a moving of the earth under me and heard a rumbling sound. . . . It seemed there was a motion to the trees around us. 'How did I like California now?' Moody asked me."[16]

Manly reported seeing herds of elk and grizzly bears in the distance eating wild blackberries. He strolled through fields of wild mustard growing taller than he was. He wrote pages about the beauty of northern California, so different from his Midwestern home.

After successfully panning for gold, Manly returned to Wisconsin in the fall of 1850 to visit his family. He carried with him ten pounds (4.54 kg) of gold dust, worth $2,000. From San Francisco, he sailed to Acapulco, Mexico, then to Panama. In those days before the Panama Canal was built, he, like all travelers, had to hike across the narrow jungle isthmus that separates the Atlantic and Pacific oceans. On the Atlantic side, another ship took Manly to Havana, Cuba, then to New Orleans. From there, he went up the Mississippi River on a steamboat, gambling along the way. Once Manly reached St. Louis, he took stagecoaches to Wisconsin.

But like other Death Valley survivors, Manly couldn't stay put for long. In a few months, he went back to California the way he'd just come. In northern California, he again visited Bennett and his children. He gave a horse to young George Bennett. Manly next visited the Arcans and found little Charlie recovered. He ran into Captain Hunt, now a respected member of the California legislature, in Sacramento. Manly again tried gold mining, then cattle ranching, and then raising pears in southern California.

Manly traveled back into Death Valley several times, and lectured about his trip through Death Valley in his later years. After he died in 1903, treasure hunters tore up his house and yard to look for the gold they were certain he had hidden there. But none was ever found.

John Rogers was a man of few words. In April 1894, he described his part in the escape from Death Valley: "We put the babies on the oxen and started for Los Angeles. Arrived there March 7, 1850, dead broke. I went to work in a black-smith shop at $1.00 per day, and after earning a few dollars all hands started for the mines. We struck the mines at Sonora.

I then drifted down to Mariposa County. And here I am, a cripple for life."[17]

Rogers and Manly lost track of each other about 1854. They met again in a tearful reunion near Merced, California, in 1895, 41 years later. By then Rogers was crippled and nearly blind. He'd inhaled mercury fumes while working in a gold mine, damaging the nerves in his feet. The injury had cost Rogers his toes, and he hobbled about with a cane. He died soon after.

Cuff, Old Crump, and the One-Eyed Mule

Cuff came through the journey and traveled to northern California with the Bennetts. When Manly visited, Cuff recognized him and happily greeted his old friend from Death Valley. In Georgetown, a small gold town outside Sacramento, Cuff was stolen, and never seen again. A miner may have recognized Cuff's intelligence and taken the dog for his own. This was a sad loss to the Bennetts. Cuff had been with them for years, and they loved him dearly.

Old Crump also survived. Manly's book about the Death Valley forty-niners mentions the goodness and sensible disposition of the ox many times. He called the animal, "Old Christian Crump."[18] Manly was pleased to find the ox grazing in a field near French Camp in 1856. He'd recognized Old Crump's crooked horn.

"He was now fat and sleek, and as kind and gentle as when so poor upon the terrible journey. I got off my horse and went up to him, and patted my old friend. I was glad to find him so contented and happy, and I doubt not that he too was glad."[19] Old Crump's new owner wouldn't sell him or let him be worked. The ox had a secure and happy retirement—a reward for his faithful duty to the Bennett and Arcan children.

Manly also valued his mule—although he apparently never named her—calling her his pet and recognizing her bravery and loyalty. "I thought a great deal of my fat little one-eyed mule. . . . and how she did her part on the fearful road to and from Death Valley."[20] He took the mule with him to northern California, and turned her loose to graze in the rich fields. Manly kept the mule until he returned to Wisconsin, when he sold her and his gun for 12 ounces (340.2 g) of gold dust to finance his travels.

CHAPTER 16

THE DEATH VALLEY HEROES

ACCOUNTS DIFFER about how many Sand Walkers died on the trip from Salt Lake City to Los Angeles, but most agree that thirteen men perished of hunger and thirst. It was reported but never verified that one unnamed Jayhawker was run out of camp when he suggested cannibalism. The horror of the Donner Party's survival story haunted the pioneers, and most said they'd rather die of hunger.

The Death Valley forty-niners were the only large group of pioneers to lose their way in the California Gold Rush. If they'd been traveling through Death Valley and the Mojave Desert during the summer instead of midwinter, none of them could have survived the cruel and punishing heat.

All the parents made great personal sacrifices to ensure their children's survival. Many of the Death Valley forty-niners performed heroic feats, like sharing meager supplies of food and water with their comrades. However, Juliet Brier and William Manly are perhaps the most obvious heroes.

The Jayhawkers considered Juliet Brier a heroine. One of them wrote about her in later years: "The strongest of the whole party was wee, nervous Mrs. Brier, who shared with her boys that indescribable tramp of 900 miles (1,449 km). For the last three weeks she had to lift her husband from the ground every morning and steady him a few moments before he could stand. She helped wasted giants who a few months before could have held her upon their palms. Her boys who'd had a bitter experience such as perhaps no other boys ever survived, were stalwart men."[1]

Another Jayhawker said about her, "She was a mother to all the Jayhawker boys when they were sick or in despair."[2] They felt that Juliet's husband and children survived solely because of her courage and fortitude.

Not only did she take care of her own family, she also helped the men as best she could. "Did I nurse the sick? Ah, there was little of that to do. I always did what I could for the poor fellows, but it wasn't much. When one grew sick, he just lay down, weary like, and his life went out. Poor souls!"[3] Today Juliet Brier lies in an unmarked grave in a country cemetery in northern California.

THE HEROISM OF William Manly and John Rogers still shines through the years. They could have easily escaped Death Valley, but instead they returned to the Bennett and Arcan families waiting in the desert for their help. Close ties of long friendship bound Manly to the Bennetts, but Rogers hadn't met the family until Hobble Creek. Yet he never hesitated to cast his lot with Manly and them.

Perhaps it was Manly's early Vermont upbringing, similar to that of Juliet Brier's, that guided his actions. Manly's mother told him when he left home as a young man, "We have striven to make you a good and honest man. You must follow our teachings and your conscience will be clear."[4] Manly did follow his conscience when he decided he must help the two families instead of leaving them to die in the desert.

William Manly wrote a book called *Death Valley in '49*. Published in 1894, the book has been widely read, and historians consider it a manuscript of remarkable accuracy and descriptive excellence. Manly's memorable first-person telling of the story of the Death Valley forty-niners is as exciting today as it was when it was first published over a century ago. Manly's comments drawn from the final pages of his book about the taming of the Old West still ring clear and true today.

> Men from every state gathered on the banks of the Missouri to set out together across the plains. These men, reared with differing ways and customs, religions and politics, made up a strange group when thrown together. But the good and true came to the surface. Some left civilization with all the luxuries money could buy. But their sleek fat horses grew thin, the wagon trains grew small, and some of them went the last 100 miles on foot, or were buried as they fell upon the sand and rocks.
>
> Those who got through to California found a splendid climate and promising prospects of filling empty pockets with yellow treasure. Those who came early cleared the way and started the great stream of gold that has made America one of the richest nations of the world. Here in this pleasant and fair land, I rest in the midst of family and friends and can truly say, I am content.[5]

The Death Valley forty-niners buried thousands of dollars in gold coins in Death Valley and the Mojave deserts when their weight became too great to carry. None of the coins have ever been recovered, although the valley has yielded up other treasures in the forms of silver and borax. Tourism is a remunerative industry. Death Valley remains a land of stark beauty and sharp contrasts, deadly dangerous in some spots, grandly glorious in others, a place for all to enjoy and respect, now and forever.

NOTES

Prologue
1. Rolle, Andrew, *California: A History, 5th Ed.* (Wheeling, IL: Harlan Davidson, 1998), 94.
2. Rolle, 96.
3. Belden, L. Burr, *Goodbye, Death Valley! The Tragic 1849 Jayhawker Trek* (Bishop, CA: Chalfant Press, 1956), 15.
4. Bloch, Louis M., Jr., ed., *Overland to California in 1859. A Guide for Wagon Train Travelers* (Cleveland, OH: Bloch and Company, 1983), 23.
5. Bloch, 20.
6. Latta, Frank, *Death Valley '49ers* (Salt Lake City, UT: Publishers Press, 1979), 57.

Chapter 1
1. Belden, L. Burr, *Death Valley Heroine and Source Accounts of the 1849 Travelers* (San Bernardino, CA: Inland Printing & Engraving Company, 1954), 26.
2. Leadingham, Grace, "Juliet Wells Brier, Heroine of Death Valley—Chapters 2 & 3," *The Pacific Historian—Quarterly Bulletin of the California History Foundation and the Jedediah Smith Society,* Vol. VIII, 1 (February, 1964), 20.
3. Johnson, Leroy and Jean, *Escape From Death Valley, as told by William Lewis Manly and Other '49ers* (Reno, NV: University of Nevada Press, 1987), 50.
4. Manly, William L., *Death Valley in '49, an important chapter of California pioneer history* (1894). (Reprinted, with a foreword by John Steven McGroarty, New York: Wallace Hebberd, 1929), 103.
5. Latta, Frank, 75.

Chapter 2

1. Brier, John W., "Death Valley Party of 1849," *Out West*, March 1903, 328.

Chapter 3

1. Ellenbecker, John G., *The Jayhawkers of Death Valley* (Marysville, KS: 1938), 25.
2. Hafen, LeRoy and Ann, eds. *Journals of Forty-Niners, Salt Lake to Los Angeles* (Glendale, CA: Arthur H. Clark, 1954), 78–79.
3. Young, Bob and Jan, *The '49ers—The Story of the California Gold Rush* (New York: Julian Messner, 1996), 101.
4. Lothrop, Gloria, *The Californians*, November/December 1984, 31.
5. Hafen, 78–79.
6. Young, 101.
7. Manly, 107.
8. Manly, 109.
9. Burrel, Louisa H., "Across the Plains in 1849," *San Jose Pioneer*, December 15, 1894, 2.
10. Brier, 328.
11. Long, Margaret, *Shadow of the Arrow* (Caldwell, ID: Caxton Printers, 1950), 173.
12. Stephens, L. Dow, *Life Sketches of a Jayhawker in '49* (San Jose, CA: Nolta Brothers, 1916), 19.
13. Belden, 27.

Chapter 4

1. Ellenbecker, John G., *The Jayhawkers of Death Valley* (Marysville, KS, 1938), 22.
2. Lothrop, 32.
3. Latta, 173.
4. Manly, 141–142.
5. Manly, 118.
6. Manly, 119.
7. Manly, 120.
8. Manly, 121–122.
9. Latta, 75.
10. Burrel, 2.
11. Johnson, 59.

12. Manly, 125.
13. Manly, 125.
14. Manly, 127.
15. Manly, 127.
16. Manly, 128.
17. Manly, 133.

Chapter 5
1. Brier, 335.
2. Belden, L. Burr, *Death Valley Heroine and Source Accounts of the 1849 Travelers* (San Bernardino, CA: Inland Printing & Engraving Company, 1954), 33.
3. Brier, 333.
4. Ellenbecker, 28.
5. Leadingham, Grace, "Juliet Wells Brier, Heroine of Death Valley—Chapter 1." *The Pacific Historian—Quarterly Bulletin of the California History Foundation and the Jedediah Smith Society*, VII 4 (November, 1963), 172.
6. Leadingham, 172.

Chapter 6
1. Belden, 21.
2. Belden, 21–22.
3. Belden, 22.
4. Belden, 22.
5. Belden, 22.
6. Belden, 22.
7. Johnson, 173.
8. Belden, 34.
9. Manly, 136.
10. Koenig, George, *The Lost Death Valley '49er Journal of Louis Nusbaumer* (Bishop, CA: Chalfant Press, 1974), frontispiece.
11. Belden, 29.
12. Belden, 29.
13. Ellenbecker, 62.

Chapter 7
1. Belden, 23.
2. Belden, 23.

3. Wheat, Carl I, "Trailing the Forty-Niners Through Death Valley," *Sierra Club Bulletin*, XXIV, No. 3, (1939), 101.
4. Johnson, 60–61.
5. Belden, 23.
6. Belden, 23.
7. Latta, 141.
8. Johnson, 182.
9. Ellenbecker, 35.

Chapter 8
1. Latta, 124.
2. Manly, 140.
3. Manly, 124.
4. Manly, 151.
5. Manly, 151.
6. Manly, 153.
7. Manly, 153–154.

Chapter 9
1. Long, 282.
2. Latta, 81.
3. Burrel, 2.
4. Manly, 205.
5. Manly, p. 206.
6. Johnson, 112.
7. Johnson, Leroy & Jean, *Julia—Death Valley's Youngest Victim*, 2 ed. (Bishop, CA, 1996), 6–8.
8. Schlissel, Lillian, *Women's Diaries of the Westward Journey* (New York: Schocken Books, 1982), 183.
9. Johnson (1987), 112.

Chapter 10
1. Belden, 24.
2. Leadingham, 173–174.
3. Belden, 25.
4. Manly, 480.
5. Latta, 179.
6. Belden, 24.

7. Latta, 179.
8. Belden, 25.
9. Wheat, 94.
10. Johnson (1987), 177.

Chapter 11
1. Belden, 25.
2. Belden, 25–26.
3. Belden, 26.
4. Belden, 26.
5. Belden, 26.
6. Brier, 456.
7. Ellenbecker, 47.
8. Ellenbecker, 107.
9. Leadingham, 19.
10. Belden, p. 27.
11. Leadingham, 177.
12. Ellenbecker, 56–57.
13. Belden, 27.
14. Belden, 27.
15. Brier, 459.
16. Brier, 459.
17. Belden, 28.
18. Brier, 459.
19. Brier, 461.
20. Brier, 462.
21. Brier, 462.
22. Brier, 463.
23. Belden, 28.

Chapter 12
1. Manly, 203.
2. Johnson (1987), 107.
3. Manly, 204.
4. Johnson (1987), 108.
5. Manly, 187.
6. Manly, 204.
7. Manly, 204.

8. Manly, 204.
9. Johnson, 109.
10. Manly, 207.
11. Manly, 196.
12. Johnson, 113.
13. Manly, 211–212.
14. Johnson, 112.
15. Johnson, 114.
16. Manly, 213–214.
17. Manly, 215.
18. Manly, 216.
19. Manly, 216.

Chapter 13
1. Manly, 218.
2. Manly, 218–219.
3. Manly, 221.
4. Belden, 35.
5. Manly, 221.
6. Manly, 477.
7. Manly, 224.
8. Manly, 225.
9. Manly, 225.
10. Manly, 226.
11. Manly, 231.
12. Manly, 242.
13. Manly, 246.
14. Manly, 252.

Chapter 14
1. Bloch, 34.
2. Burrel, 2.
3. Burrel, 2.
4. Latta, 186.
5. Manly, 267.
6. Manly, 267.
7. Manly, 270.
8. Manly, 272.

9. Manly, 272.
10. Manly, 277.
11. Manly, 277.
12. Manly, 278.

Chapter 15
1. Brier, John W., "Death Valley Party of 1849, concluded," *Out West*, (April, 1903), 463.
2. Manly, 284.
3. Brier, 463.
4. Johnson (1987), 180.
5. Johnson, 180.
6. Ellenbecker, 22.
7. Latta, 138.
8. Stephens, 24.
9. Levy, Joann, *They Saw the Elephant—Women in the California Gold Rush,* (Hamden, CT: Archon Books, 1990), 29.
10. Johnson (1996), 6.
11. Belden, L. Burr, *The Wade Story: In and Out of Death Valley,* (San Bernardino, CA: Inland Printing & Engraving Company, 1957), 9.
12. Manly, 282.
13. Manly, 282.
14. Manly, 285.
15. Manly, 288.
16. Manly, 297.
17. Latta, 339.
18. Manly, 230.
19. Manly, 389.
20. Manly, 319.

Chapter 16
1. Belden, p. 16-17.
2. Ellenbecker, 41.
3. Belden, 27.
4. Manly, 24.
5. Manly, 518–524.

FOR FURTHER READING

Belden, L. Burr. *Death Valley Heroine and Source Accounts of the 1849 Travelers*. San Bernardino, CA: Inland Printing & Engraving Company, 1954.

Belden, L. Burr. *Goodbye, Death Valley! The Tragic 1849 Jayhawker Trek*. Bishop, CA: Chalfant Press, Inc., 1956.

Belden, L. Burr. *The Wade Story: In and Out of Death Valley*. San Bernardino, CA: Inland Printing & Engraving Company, 1957.

"Biographical Sketches—W. L. Manly." *San Jose Pioneer* (April 21, 1877; April 28, 1877), 1.

Bloch, Louis M., Jr., Ed. *Overland to California in 1859. A Guide for Wagon Train Travelers*. Cleveland, OH: Bloch and Co., 1983.

Brier, John W. "Death Valley Party of 1849." *Out West* (March 1903), 326–335.

Brier, John W. "Death Valley Party of 1849, concluded." *Out West* (April 1903), 456–465.

Burrel, Louisa H. "Across the Plains in 1849." *San Jose Pioneer* (December 15, 1894), 2.

Ellenbecker, John G. *The Jayhawkers of Death Valley*. Marysville, KS: 1938.

Erickson, Paul. *Daily Life in a Covered Wagon*. Washington, DC: Preservation Press (National Trust for Historic Preservation), 1994.

Gray, Dorothy K. *Women of the West*. Millbrae, CA: Les Femmes, 1976.

Hafen, LeRoy and Ann, Eds. *Journals of Forty-Niners, Salt Lake to Los Angeles*. Glendale, CA: Arthur H. Clark Co., 1954.

Jackson, Donald Dale. *Gold Dust—The Saga of the Forty Niners*. New York: Alfred A. Knopf, 1980.

Johnson, Leroy and Jean. *Escape From Death Valley*. Reno, NV: University of Nevada Press, 1987.

Johnson, Leroy and Jean. *Julia—Death Valley's Youngest Victim*, 2nd Ed. Bishop, CA: 1996.

Koenig, George. *The Lost Death Valley '49er Journal of Louis Nusbaumer*. Bishop, CA: Chalfant Press, 1974.

Latta, Frank. *Death Valley '49ers*. Salt Lake City, UT: Publishers Press, 1979.

Laycock, George. *Death Valley*. New York: Four Winds Press, 1976.

Leadingham, Grace. "Juliet Wells Brier, Heroine of Death Valley— Chapter 1." *The Pacific Historian—Quarterly Bulletin of the California History Foundation and the Jedediah Smith Society*, VII (4) (November 1963), 171–178.

Leadingham, Grace. "Juliet Wells Brier, Heroine of Death Valley— Chapters 2 & 3." *The Pacific Historian—Quarterly Bulletin of the California History Foundation and the Jedediah Smith Society*, VIII (1) (February 1964), 13–20.

Levy, Joann. *They Saw the Elephant—Women in the California Gold Rush*. Hamden, CT: Archon Books, 1990.

Lingenfelter, Richard. *Death Valley and the Amargosa*. Berkeley, CA: University of California Press, 1986.

Long, Margaret. *Shadow of the Arrow*. Caldwell, ID: Caxton Printers, 1950.

Lothrop, Gloria. *The Californians*. November/December, 31–35, 1984.

Lummis, Charles F. *Strange Corners of our Country*. New York: Century Company, 1900.

Manly, William L. *Death Valley in '49, an important chapter of California pioneer history* [1894]. Reprint, foreword by John Steven McGroarty. New York: Wallace Hebberd, 1929.

Manly, William L. "The Original Jayhawkers." *San Jose Pioneer* (March 15, 1894), 2.

Rolle, Andrew. *California: A History*, 5th Edition. Wheeling, IL: Harlan Davidson, 1998.

Schlissel, Lillian. *Women's Diaries of the Westward Journey*. New York: Schocken Books, 1982.

Stefoff, Rebecca. *Children of the Westward Trail*. Brookfield, CT: The Millbrook Press, 1996.

Stephens, L. Dow. *Life Sketches of a Jayhawker in '49*. San Jose, CA: Nolta Brothers, 1916.

Wheat, Carl I. "Trailing the Forty-Niners Through Death Valley." *Sierra Club Bulletin*, XXIV, 3, (1939).

Young, Bob and Jan. *The '49ers—The Story of the California Gold Rush*. New York: Julian Messner, 1996.

INDEX

Trona, 78
Trona Pinnacles, *79*

Wade, Almira, 19, *21*, 35,
    107–111, 123
Wade, Charles, 19, 123
Wade, Harry George, 19, 20, 66,
    108, 109, 122
Wade, Henry, 19, 35, 66,
    107–109, 122–123
Wade, Mary, 19, *21*, 57, 58, 66,
    122, 123

Wade, Mary Ann, 122
Wade, Richard, 19, *21*, 107,
    123
Wade family, 24, 25, 29–31,
    33–35, 37, 45, 57, 58, 60, 66,
    107–111, 122–123
Walkara, Chief, 27–28
Walkara map, 27–29, 34
Wells, Hiram, 13
Wheat, Carl, 53

Young, Brigham, 23, 24